Also by John Shook

Learning to See: Value-Stream Mapping to Add Value and Eliminate Muda

Kaizen Express

ISBN 978-1-934109-20-5
Design by Off-Piste Design

Lean Enterprise Institute, Inc.
215 First Street, Suite 300
Cambridge, MA 02142 USA
(t) 617-871-2900 • (f) 617-871-2999 • lean.org

Managing to Learn

Using the A3 management process to solve problems, gain agreement, mentor, and lead

by John Shook

Foreword by Jim Womack

Lean Enterprise Institute
Cambridge, MA, USA
lean.org

Version 1.1
July 2010

Acknowledgments

I'm indebted to more people who helped make this book possible than I can possibly thank.

My debt of gratitude begins with my many mentors at Toyota. Whatever I have learned about management and the A3 process owes everything to them. For my first managers, Isao Yoshino and Ken Kunieda, teaching me the A3 process wasn't merely an act of kindness on their part—they desperately needed me to learn the thinking and gain the skills so I could begin to make myself useful. From learning as a novice under their guidance to years later assisting Mike Masaki address the challenge of introducing A3 thinking to an organization of American engineers, my mentors have been many and my learning constant.

I also have many to thank for specific help in writing this book. Mathew Lovejoy, Scott Heydon, Lynn Kelly, Eric Ethington, Cindy Swank, and Jerry Bussell each provided insightful and critical feedback from the perspective of executives learning to use the process to make real progress in their companies.

Jack Billi and Denise Bennett helped me appreciate the powerful role the A3 process can play in introducing lean thinking to complex healthcare organizations. The manuscript itself benefited greatly and specifically from Jack's insights and red pen.

Durward Sobek, Art Smalley, and Mike Rother were all, coincidentally, writing manuscripts on related topics at the same time; this book grew more than a little from our ongoing discussions and collaborations. Richard Whiteside and Terry Vigdorth provided commentary challenging both the concepts and the presentation that was valuable in shaping the story.

David Verble and Jeff Smith, two fellow ex-Toyota colleagues with whom I have shared this learning journey for many years, read the manuscript and provided predictably critical and, therefore, especially valuable feedback: Your names both appear briefly elsewhere within these pages—they could appear on each page.

Thanks, too, for critical feedback from Tom Waters and Tim Andree, fellow veterans of A3 wars from years we spent together on the front lines of Toyota in Japan back in the 1980s.

Of course, collaboration from the Lean Enterprise Institute community has been instrumental. David Brunt and Dan Jones of the Lean Enterprise Academy UK provided valuable critique, while Jose Ferro, Flavio Picchi, and Gilberto Kosaka at the Lean Institute Brasil are already hard at work on the Portuguese translation! Special thanks are due to Dave LaHote, Dave Logozzo, and Helen Zak for ongoing support and encouragement on this and other collaborations, as well as LEI staff who offered their critiques through the process. Michael Brassard provided advice, critique, debate, and insights—this book would not be what it is without the support you provided.

The editorial team of George Taninecz, Tom Ehrenfeld, and Thomas Skehan made hard work fun, fun work productive, and productive work rewarding. I hope you are ready for Round Two.

Jim Womack deserves special gratitude for his encouraging and cajoling to write this book to begin with. Jim often states that the most significant help he provides individuals along their lean journey (a phrasing that Jim hates, and I therefore gleefully use here) is to simply provide them with courage: In this case, at least, there would be no book were it not for Jim's encouragement.

Most of all, this is dedicated to my son Jesse, a lieutenant in the United States Marine Corp, and daughter Saya, going to school full-time and working full-time in Tokyo; you don't know how much you inspired me as I was writing this. This is for you, as you embark on your own journeys of life and learning to destinations unknown.

John Shook

Foreword

I'm enormously excited about this book. John Shook's *Managing to Learn* seeks to answer a simple but profound question: What is at the heart of lean management and lean leadership?

In addressing this question, *Managing to Learn* helps fill in the gap between our understanding of lean tools, such as value-stream mapping, and *the sustainable application of these tools*. In the process it reveals:

- The distinction between old-fashioned, top-down, command-and-control management and lean management.
- The difference between an organization based on *authority* and one based on *responsibility*.
- The enduring benefits realized by managers who dig deep in the details to discover root causes rather than jumping to solutions.
- The power of creating lean managers and leaders *through* the process of solving problems and implementing plans.

Managing to Learn shines a bright light on the many dimensions by which the lean method is superior to today's dominant approach to management and to leadership (which are often nothing more than firefighting). Perhaps most extraordinarily, this book shows how this better method of management is taught and learned through dialogue about concrete problems. It does this by means of a dialogue between a lean manager and a subordinate who learns lean management and leadership as he solves an important problem.

This process of solving problems while creating better employees—A3 analysis—is core to the Toyota management system. An A3 report guides the dialogue and analysis. It identifies the current situation, the nature of the issue, the range of possible countermeasures, the best countermeasure, the means (who will do what when) to put it into practice, and the evidence that the issue has actually been addressed.

This volume describes A3 analysis and provides examples of how to use the tool. But its truly important contribution is to explain the thought process behind the tool—A3 thinking. Indeed, A3 thinking turns routine managing into cumulative learning for the whole organization. Hence the title, *Managing to Learn*.

Because A3 thinking is so different from conventional management thinking, only someone who actually has experienced it as an employee and deployed it as a manager can fully explain its nuances. John is therefore the ideal author. He was hired in 1983 as an employee at Toyota in Japan, where he learned A3 as the pupil, the deshi. As he became a manager he practiced A3 as the teacher, the sensei. At the same time, he was still the deshi of higher-level mangers, whose core management tasks included teaching additional aspects of A3 analysis to everyone they managed.

John's job eventually became to help manage the transfer of Toyota's lean management system across the world. He began this work at the NUMMI joint venture with General Motors in 1984, and continued with the startup of Toyota's Georgetown facility in 1986. Next, he transferred to Toyota's rapidly expanding North American engineering center in Ann Arbor, MI, and then finished his Toyota career helping launch the Toyota Supplier Support Center in Kentucky. At every stop he taught A3 thinking by mentoring younger managers and employees, and continued his own learning through A3 dialogue with his superiors. Since leaving Toyota he has taught these principles to organizations across the world.

John's book is a unique achievement in explaining a vital management tool while at the same time revealing the thought process behind its use. To achieve this dual purpose the book employs a unique layout. The thoughts and actions of the lower-level manager are on the left side of the page and the simultaneous thoughts and actions of the higher-level supervisor are on the right side. You will see a learning process unfolding as a complex problem is solved and a new lean manager is created.

The transition to A3 management is a major leap for all of us. It demands that we manage by PDCA (plan, do, check, act), the scientific method, and science is hard work. We all want to jump to conclusions about what to do, and then be given the freedom as managers to "just do it." Yet A3 thinking continually pulls us toward a much more constructive reality. There we look hard at the current situation, dig deep to discover the root cause of problems, consider many countermeasures (not just the most obvious "solution"), rigorously lay out an implementation plan, and carefully collect data to see if our countermeasure has really improved the situation. And then we repeat this cycle.

In *Managing to Learn*, John has captured the thought process behind lean management and leadership. And he has provided the methods you will need to succeed with A3 analysis. This way of thinking is essential to gaining and sustaining the benefits of the lean tools you have already mastered.

We are eager to hear about your successes as well as your difficulties. Please contact us and John by sending your comments and questions to *mtl@lean.org*. With a bit of practice and a lot of perseverance, we can all manage to learn.

Jim Womack
Chairman, Lean Enterprise Institute
October 2008

Contents

Introduction

At Toyota, where I worked for more than 10 years, the way of thinking about problems and learning from them for more effective planning, decision-making, and execution is one of the secrets of the company's success. The process by which the company identifies, frames, and then acts on problems and challenges at all levels—perhaps the key to its entire system of developing talent and continually deepening its knowledge and capabilities—can be found in the structure of its A3 process.

And so this book is designed to help you learn from your problems as you seek to solve them, while at the same time producing innovative and problem-solving employees. Many elements of the Toyota system have been held up as the key to its tremendous success, but the most important accomplishment of the company is simply that it has *learned to learn*.

Many people familiar with A3 reports see them primarily as a simple communication tool or problem-solving technique. It's understandable that they focus on this immediate, though limited, application. A3s are, indeed, powerful tools that lead to effective countermeasures based on facts. As a result, companies that successfully implement them for decision-making, planning, proposals, and problem-solving can realize instant gains.

But in this book I also want to reveal A3 as a *management process*. The widespread adoption of the A3 process standardizes a methodology for innovating, planning, problem-solving, and building foundational structures for sharing a broader and deeper form of thinking. This produces organizational learning that is deeply rooted in the work itself—operational learning.

Discovery at Toyota

I discovered the A3 process of managing to learn firsthand during the natural course of my work in Toyota City beginning in 1983. I was mentored and saw my Japanese colleagues both being mentored and mentoring others in the company's most prevalent management tool—its most visible form of organizational "currency." My colleagues and I wrote A3s almost daily. We would joke, and lament, that it seemed we would regularly rewrite A3s 10 times or more. We would write and revise them, tear them up and start over, discuss them and curse them, all as ways of clarifying our own thinking, learning from others, informing and teaching others, capturing lessons learned, hammering down decisions, and reflecting on what was going on.

Every year I saw new Toyota recruits, just graduated from the university, arrive at their desks to find a blank sheet of A3-sized paper, a mentor, and a problem or project for which they were assigned ownership. Over the course of the first months, each would be coached through A3 thinking. They explored how to "go see" and comprehend the real nature of a problem, how to analyze it, and how to take effective initiative to *work the organization* to develop reasonable countermeasures to improve the situation.

My own epiphany came when my boss told me, "Never tell your staff exactly what to do. Whenever you do that, you take responsibility away from them." His comments revealed how Toyota operates not as an "authority-based" but a "responsibility-based" organization. Almost all organizations (certainly *all* large ones) are cross-functional in operation while being functional in structure. This results in a matrix that so often leaves ownership unclear, decision-making stymied, and everyone frustrated.

Pull-Based Authority

In stark contrast, effective use of the A3 process can facilitate the shift from a *debate* about who owns what (an authority-focused debate) to a *dialogue* around *what is the right thing to do* (a responsibility-focused conversation). This shift has a radical impact on the way decisions are made. Individuals earn the authority to take action through the manner in which they frame the issue. They form consensus and get decisions made by focusing relentlessly on indisputable facts that they and their peers derive from the gemba.

However, for leaders to refrain—as much as possible—from dictating does *not* mean laissez-faire disengagement. As we shall see, the Toyota leader engages in the messy details of the work being done in order to learn and become thoroughly knowledgeable about the process at hand. Questioning, coaching, and teaching take precedence over commanding and controlling. That's why Toyota pioneer Taiichi Ohno believed that one could learn what's important about an operation by simply standing and observing it from one fixed location. Where the laissez-faire, hands-off manager will content himself to set targets and delegate everything, essentially saying, "I don't care how you do it, as long as you get the results," the Toyota manager desperately wants to know how you'll do it, saying, "I want to hear everything about your thinking, tell me about your plans." Only then can the manager mentor the problem-solver.

Therefore decision-making and actions are interwoven with planning and problem-solving. The manager's job is to see problems, and he can only do so by knowing every messy detail of the work being done—the A3s of those working with him contain these facts. It is assumed that there will be problems, and that nothing will go according to plan. That's why Toyota managers are known to say, "No problem is problem." This recognizes that it is the very job of all managers—even all employees—to see and respond to the problems that are there, the problems that we *know* must be there. By successfully incorporating the A3 into team activities, companies will not only learn to stop avoiding problems, they will begin to recognize problems as powerful opportunities for learning and for improvement.

Unlike traditional command-and-control leaders who rely on the authority of their position to instruct others how to deploy strategy, the Toyota leader is concerned more with responsibility. The Toyota leader will strive whenever possible to eschew simple command in favor of leading by being knowledgeable, fact-based, and strong-willed yet flexible; in other words, by being a true *leader*.

But, just as this leader eschews command and control, he also embraces a style and process that contrasts equally with the laissez-faire, hands-off approach of the supposedly enlightened modern manager. This is a stark contrast to the results-only-oriented, management-by-numbers approach—often couched in the misleading terms of "management by objectives"—that is employed by many conventional managers. As H. Thomas Johnson noted,[1] whereas the traditional manager tries to manage by manipulating results—something akin to driving while looking in the rearview mirror—Toyota managers manage the means, the process itself that actually leads to results.

As a result, Toyota management can best be understood as neither "top-down" nor "bottom-up." The A3 process clarifies responsibility by placing ownership squarely on the shoulders of the author-owner of the A3, the individual whose initials appear in the upper right-hand corner of the paper. This person may not have direct authority over every aspect of the proposal. Yet this owner is clearly identified as the person who has taken or accepted responsibility *to get decisions made and implemented.*

While it would be an overstatement to say that the entire Toyota management system boils down to this one method (not every Toyota manager exhibits all these characteristics all the time), it's fair to say that effective use of the A3 can embody the extraordinary management thinking that has made Toyota what it is.

At Toyota, there was never a stated goal to "implement the A3 process." Rather, the A3 emerged as the method through which it could yoke two important work management processes: hoshin kanri (strategy management) and problem-solving. At the macro enterprise level, hoshin kanri aligns organizational goals and objectives with operations and activities, while at the micro, or individual level, formalized problem-solving creates operational learning. The A3 process combines and embodies both. As a result, companies that seek a disciplined hoshin kanri process and an effective problem-solving process will find tremendous challenge and opportunity in embracing the A3 process.

1. H. Thomas Johnson, *Lean Dilemma: Choose System Principles or Management Accounting Controls, Not Both*, self-published paper and a winner of the 2007 Shingo Research Award, Sept. 26, 2006.

At companies on a lean journey, individuals at every level can use A3s as a way to propose projects, take initiative, show ownership, sell ideas, gain agreement, and learn. Managers can use A3 thinking to coach and teach; to assign clear responsibility, ownership, and accountability; to get good plans from subordinates; and to mentor employees. And organizations can use A3 thinking to get decisions made, to achieve objectives and get things done, to align people and teams along common goals, and, above all, to learn for effectiveness, efficiency, and improvement. A3 works as both a problem-solving tool and as a structured process for creating problem-solvers. The A3 helps spread a scientific method that forces individuals to observe reality, present data, propose a working countermeasure designed to achieve the stated goal, and follow up with a process of checking and adjusting for actual results.

This Book

You're holding a book within a book: one to share the fundamentals of the tool, and a second to share the underlying learning process.

The core story shares how young manager Desi Porter, who is versed in lean basics, discovers the content and meaning of the A3 process. As he learns, you will become familiar with some typical formal elements of an A3 proposal and its applications. Porter's story appears on the left side of each page in black text. The story of Porter's A3 education is deeply informed by its counterpart, which reveals the thinking behind the actions and insights of his supervisor, Ken Sanderson, as he mentors our protagonist through the learning process. Sanderson's story appears in blue text on the right side of the page.

Mentor Sanderson seeks to apply this broader approach to his own set of problems and decisions. He understands that the A3 process illustrates the means to build robust, sensible systems and processes that cascade responsibility throughout the organization. The intent is to embed organizational habits, practices, and mindsets that enable, encourage, and teach people to think and to take initiative. The system is based on building structured opportunities for people to learn in the manner that comes most naturally to them: through experience, learning from mistakes, and plan-based trial and error.

So the goals for this book are both modest and ambitious.

In this book, you will learn how to write an A3 proposal. Writing an A3 is the first step toward learning to use the A3 process, toward *learning to learn.* Some benefits in improved problem-solving, decision-making, and communications ability can be expected when individual A3 authors adopt this approach. But unless the broader organization embraces the broader process, the much greater benefit will be unrealized. The entire effort may degenerate into a "check-the-box" exercise, as A3s will join unused SPC charts, ignored standardized work forms, and disregarded value-stream maps as corporate wallpaper.

Every organization I know struggles to incorporate and sustain successful operations along these principles. The A3 is but a tool in a broader system. My hope is that by applying the practices of both the core story and its management perspectives that managers and supervisors can improve their lean learning and leadership. The real questions that should precede your reading of this book are, "How do you want to manage? How do you want to lead?"

If you want to manage and lead in ways that build robust systems and processes that cascade responsibility and learning throughout the organization, then the A3 management style and process—not just the A3 piece of paper—will help you do so.

John Shook
Ann Arbor, MI, USA
October 2008

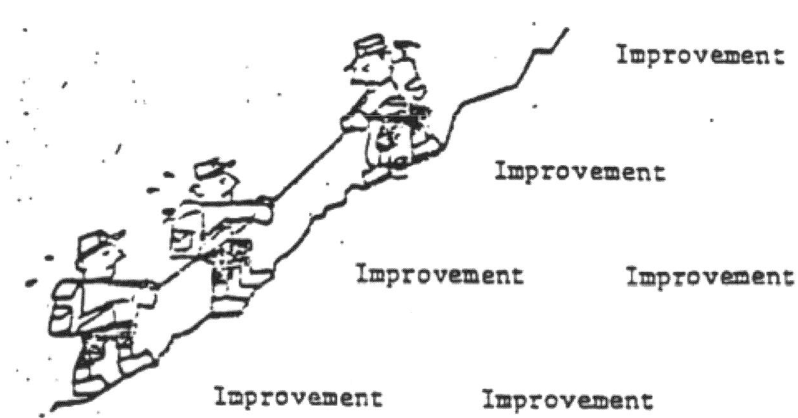

Reprinted with permission from Toyota.

The lean leader's job is to develop people. If the worker hasn't learned, the teacher hasn't taught.[2]

2. *Training Within Industry Report* (Washington, DC: War Manpower Commission, Bureau of Training, 1945).

Chapter 1
What Is an A3?

The term "A3" refers to an international-size piece of paper, one that is approximately 11-by-17 inches. Within Toyota and other lean companies, the term means much more.

Toyota's insight many years ago was that every issue an organization faces can and should be captured on a single sheet of paper. This enables everyone touching the issue to see through the same lens. While the basic thinking for an A3 (*see pages 8–9*) follows a common logic, the precise format and wording are flexible, and most organizations tweak the design to fit their unique requirements.

The A3 is like a résumé that can be adapted in layout, style, and emphasis according to the person seeking the job and the type of job being sought. Practitioners can adapt the format to fit the requirements of each situation.

On a single page, an A3 typically includes the following elements:

- *Title*—Names the problem, theme, or issue.
- *Owner/Date*—Identifies who "owns" the problem or issue and the date of the latest revision.
- *Background*—Establishes the business context and importance of the issue.
- *Current Conditions*—Describes what is currently known about the problem or issue.
- *Goals/Targets*—Identifies the desired outcome.
- *Analysis*—Analyzes the situation and the underlying causes that have created the gap between the current situation and the desired outcome.
- *Proposed Countermeasures*—Proposes some corrective actions or countermeasures to address the problem, close the gap, or reach a goal.
- *Plan*—Prescribes an action plan of who will do what when in order to reach the goal.
- *Followup*—Creates a followup review/learning process and anticipates remaining issues.

A3 Template

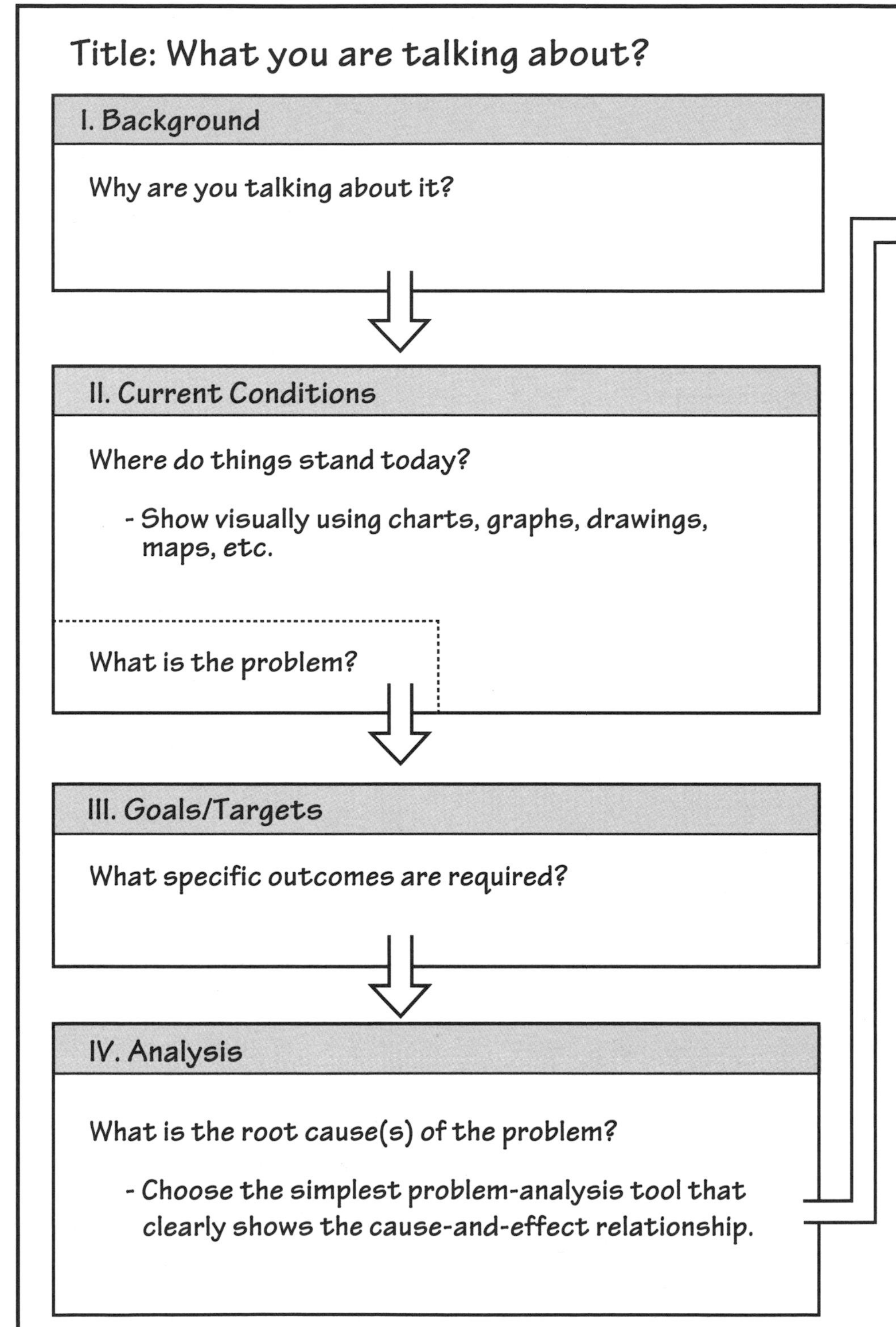

Source: John Shook and David Verble

Owner/Date				

V. Proposed Countermeasures

What is your proposal to reach the future state, the target condition?

How will your recommended countermeasures affect the root cause to achieve the target?

VI. Plan

What activities will be required for implementation and who will be responsible for what and when?

What are the indicators of performance or progress?

- Incorporate a Gantt chart or similar diagram that shows actions/outcomes, timeline, and responsibilities. May include details on specific means of implementation.

VII. Followup

What issues can be anticipated?

- Ensure ongoing PDCA.
- Capture and share learning.

These A3 elements follow one another in a natural and logical sequence. The links among the problem, its root causes, the goal, the actions proposed to achieve the goal, and the means of judging success are clear and easy to understand.

The format and the goals of the A3 are guided by the following set of questions:

1. What is the problem or issue?
2. Who owns the problem?
3. What are the root causes of the problem?
4. What are some possible countermeasures?
5. How will you decide which countermeasures to propose?
6. How will you get agreement from everyone concerned?
7. What is your implementation plan—who, what, when, where, how?
8. How will you know if your countermeasures work?
9. What followup issues can you anticipate? What problems may occur during implementation?
10. How will you capture and share the learning?

It can't be stressed enough that there's no one fixed, correct template for an A3. To illustrate this point, the back pocket of this book contains several A3 examples illustrating some of the problems, proposals, decisions, projects, plans, and issues they can address. The author decides what to emphasize depending on the specific situation and context. It is not the format of the report that matters, but the underlying thinking that leads the participants through a cycle of PDCA (plan, do, check, act).

As you will read in the coming pages, completing and then discussing the material in an A3 forces individuals to observe reality, present facts, propose working countermeasures designed to achieve the stated goal, gain agreement, and follow up with a process of checking and adjusting for actual results. As a result, the A3 represents a *powerful tool* for problem-solving, making improvements, and getting things done.

But more than that, the A3 is a visual manifestation of a problem-solving thought process involving continual dialogue between the owner of an issue and others in an organization. It is a foundational *management process* that enables and encourages learning through the scientific method. A3 reports should become a standardized form of currency for problem-solving, dialogue, and decision-making in your organization—creating an organization of scientists who continually improve operations and results through constant learning from the work at hand.

To help make that happen, the nuances of A3 as a problem-solving or improvement tool *and* a management process will be explored in the coming chapters. Together we will move through the sequence of the A3 process. In doing so, we'll see that significant work can lead to significant organizational reward.

Learning to Converse—How to Read the Following Chapters

The following five chapters have an unusual structure. Just as real dialogue in the real world is a dynamic exchange between (at least) two individuals, you will find two conversants represented in two parallel columns. On the left in black text is the main storyline and dialogue as experienced through the perspective of Desi Porter, a young manager struggling with a new assignment. On the right side in blue text, you will find running commentary that reflects the thinking of Porter's boss, Ken Sanderson, as he endeavors to mentor his young charge through the A3 learning journey.

The perspectives of Porter and Sanderson are shared side-by-side to illustrate the natural tension that characterizes any work relationship and situation. Through Porter and Sanderson's ongoing dialogue, you will see how the A3 is an emerging reflection of the conversation that it both creates and is created by.

You may choose to read the left column first and follow it through to the end of each subchapter, and then go back and read the right column. Conversely, you may read them almost at the same time, switching back and forth, dynamically—like a real conversation. Try both ways—choose whichever fits you best. Eventually you will find a rhythm that brings the dialogue of Porter and Sanderson and their learnings to life.

Chapter 2
Grasp the Situation—Go to the Gemba

Acme Manufacturing is the U.S. subsidiary of a midsized Japanese manufacturing company. Five years ago the parent company launched its initial U.S. investment with the launch of its largest overseas factory. A current expansion plan for that plant is projected to double capacity and extend product lines. The expansion also will nearly double the size of the production organization.

At the U.S. Acme site, manager Ken Sanderson has assigned middle manager Desi Porter the project of improving the document-translation process for the expansion. This translation process was fraught with problems during the plant's startup, and, now with Sanderson's mentoring, Porter has been charged with bringing such problems to light and proposing ways to improve the process. This seems simple enough, but for many companies, with the exception of those like Toyota, looking for problems is counter to corporate culture.

"For Americans and anyone, it can be a shock to the system to be actually expected to make problems visible," said Ms. Newton, a 38-year-old Indiana native who joined Toyota 15 years ago and works at North American headquarters in Erlanger, Ky. "Other corporate environments tend to hide problems from bosses."[1]

1. Martin Fackler, "'The Toyota Way' is translated for a new generation of foreign managers," *The New York Times*, February 15, 2007.

Desi Porter: What Is the Problem?

Desi Porter, a recently appointed middle manager of Acme Manufacturing, had a problem.

He stared at the blank piece of paper in front of him. He thought he knew what to do about the assignment he had just been given. But what was he really supposed to do with this piece of paper?

The assignment had been handed to him by his boss, Ken Sanderson: "Desi, the plant expansion will require a significant amount of documentation from our mother plant in Japan. Those documents will all need to be translated on-time, within budget, and with perfect quality in order to support a successful launch. I need you to look at our current translation process, evaluate it, and make a recommendation. You know the overall expansion timeline. This is very important for the company. Please prepare a preliminary A3 and bring it to me for discussion."

Porter was new to his role as junior manager of administration, but he had worked long enough within Acme's lean system to understand that a commonly accepted way of tackling problems and making proposals did exist—the A3. He had seen many A3s in his previous assignments and had, in fact, created a few simple problem-solving A3s. The format in those cases was pretty straightforward.

Porter remembered hearing one training specialist refer to A3s as "storyboards," indicating that there was a story told through a highly standardized format of panels or boxes with subject headings. Sometimes these were drawn on an 11-by-17-inch sheet of paper like he was staring at now. At other times they were large presentation panels.

Ken Sanderson: The Means to Manage

Ken Sanderson, Desi Porter's manager, had many problems.

The document translation process was just one of them. Among other things, he was responsible for reducing overall costs by 10%; improving safety in the wake of a major accident; hitting startup quality and volume numbers for the expansion; as well as addressing the many concerns that invariably arise regularly from below (the shopfloor) and above (senior leadership). On any day, people and problems were coming at him from all directions.

Sanderson had been supervising a staff of 10 direct-reports in charge of various shared services, such as purchasing and training, when he received the assignment to lead the new expansion project. The project would consume two years and $250 million, and he was gradually feeling overwhelmed. Now, with only a little more than a year to go before launch, his numerous responsibilities were growing, often without commensurate funding, he fretted, to support them.

Tight cost expectations, stringent requirements for quality, and an extremely tight timeline for the product launch were front and center. But Sanderson knew that Acme was not a

Porter knew his new assignment meant he had been given ownership of a problem, and he needed to develop a proposal. This particular problem was tied to the addition of manufacturing capacity, which would entail the construction of a new building, installation of new equipment, and hiring and training of new employees. While the expansion was great news (it confirmed that the company was doing well), the development also would create new challenges. The many difficulties of the original plant startup were still fresh in everyone's mind. One of these problems was an almost invisible but troublesome issue: translating a mountain of documents from Japanese to English.

As Porter researched the translation process, he realized that translating the documents was a huge project with complex technical requirements. It was far more complex and difficult than he had realized. The documents to be translated covered everything from the sourcing of specific parts to equipment specifications to shipping and packaging requirements. They contained highly technical terms and local idiomatic phrases, not to mention symbols and charts that were often complex and needed to be physically incorporated into the documents. Translating them quickly and accurately was essential for the plant to operate effectively at startup.

This was a complex project that touched many different operations and functions, even cultural differences. With so many requirements on so many levels, Porter wondered how he could propose the *right* solution.

He had read through an array of A3s that had been used in the plant for a variety of problems: reducing injuries from handling sheet metal, company to let budget estimates, which after all are just estimates, become the tail that wags the dog. Acme was extremely cost-conscious, but at the same time didn't fall into the trap of trying to manage by the numbers. He needed to do everything possible to control and even lower cost.

Document translation had been a back-burner issue that no one had turned serious attention to until recently. Sanderson knew that the translation process, like many others, needed to support the launch effectively by providing required levels of quality in the required time. If he could get the process to be dependable, the rest would take care of itself.

Most of Sanderson's staff had enough background in basic lean principles and tools to understand how they worked. Yet, like Porter, they often lacked enough direct experience in daily operations to see how the tools fit into a broader lean management system. And every lean skill developed from a learn-through-doing process, requiring direct, hands-on experience.

The expansion project could give many of his staff that experience. Sanderson needed to develop *the thinking* of Porter and the others. In doing so, he would develop many sets of skilled eyes and hands to support his role as a manager and leader.

producing more orderly workstations, fixing technical problems in engineering, improving invoicing and accounts receivables, and improving the customer call center in the front office. Surely this approach could help with the problem at hand.

And so, with a little knowledge, Porter earnestly began his A3 to address the document translation problem.

And so, with a mixture of trepidation and confidence, Sanderson had determined to assign this important project to Porter and mentor him to success.

Standardized Storytelling

An A3 should tell a story that anyone can understand, following it from the upper left-hand side to the lower-right side of the paper. The reports don't merely state a goal or define a problem in a static or isolated manner. Like any narrative tale, an A3 shares a complete story. There is a beginning, a middle, and an end, in which the specific elements are linked, sequential, and causal. That's why a complete A3 traces a journey from the context and definition to its "resolution," which usually prompts a sequel.

One way to describe the A3 is as "standardized storytelling," which refers to the ability of A3s to communicate both facts and meaning in a commonly understood format. Because readers are familiar with the format (a story), they can focus easily on the matter contained within as the basis for dialogue. A story is more than lifeless data to prove a point. It brings the facts and the total reality of the condition to life so the reader can understand and debate the true nature of the situation.

Not So Fast

Porter wanted to show Sanderson that he could quickly produce a quality A3 that solved the problem of translating technical documents. He wanted to complete an A3 that would get approved right away and get his solution into action.

Porter considered the basic questions and drew a template on the paper. He knew the typical A3 setup and had heard A3 proposals referred to as "standardized storytelling" (*see sidebar on p. 16*). So he tried thinking of his story, starting with the *Title* or theme. The *Title* should describe the specific problem being addressed and answer the basic question: *What does the A3 owner want to talk about, to propose?*

One of Porter's colleagues had shared this piece of A3 advice: "The *Title* is more than just a descriptive label. That's because articulating the right theme will force you to describe the real problem. Seeing the right problem and defining it accurately is the key to the entire process. You may not start with the right theme, but you will begin the conversation that gets you there."

What was the real problem that Porter needed to address? Across the top of the page he wrote, *Create robust process for translating documents.*

Porter considered the next section, the *Background* to this problem. He knew that in this first blank box he should provide the underlying conditions for the report, describing the need for the problem to be solved. *Why am I posing this problem? What is the broader business context of the issue?*

Producing People before Products

Sanderson knew that his own proficiency at putting out fires wouldn't grow his employees, produce valuable learning, or make his life any easier. Indeed, the better he got at quickly patching up a problem, the more long-term goals would elude Acme.

Sanderson needed to develop proficient problem-solvers. This meant individuals who were comfortable with a scientific approach to work, who took ownership and responsibility for their work, and who would one day have enough mastery to teach these principles to their subordinates. And he needed to make this happen without forcing it to happen. That meant there would be some mistakes along the way, but mistakes that would lead to learning.

Sanderson needed Porter and others to *learn how to learn.* The A3 would help this happen. For Sanderson, A3 represented a management process to develop learning among employees in addition to being the tool that would help Porter propose countermeasures to his specific document-translation problem.

Improving the document-translation process had not originally been high on Sanderson's radar screen. Other things, such as safety or quality, always seemed more urgent.

He knew that problems with translated Japanese documents had created numerous headaches for the plant in the past. They often arrived late and contained errors due to the complexity of translating both language and technical details. The activity was always over budget. And the problems caused by the delays and the missing information cascaded into major delays at the start of production—an unacceptable condition to allow to continue at a company like Acme.

He considered whether he could fix it by simply improving the way things were handled at the moment. Couldn't people just do their jobs better?

Porter knew that cost pressures were increasing on the company in general and that the launch plan included requirements for cost reductions in all activities. A deep dive into the cost structure of the document-translation process seemed like a good place to start, so Porter spoke with Frances, the procurement specialist in charge of purchasing indirect services such as translation.

Frances told Porter that she had been concerned about the substantial difference in the pricing of the three main translation vendors for some time. Porter prodded her for more information. As they explored this topic further, Frances looked through her files, and together they realized that the vendors had never been through a full competitive bid process. Porter was excited by this discovery, which led him to what he considered the obvious answer: implement a competitive bid process to select the best and lowest-cost vendor.

Porter immediately returned to his A3. In the box marked *Background*, he wrote, "New domestic plant expansion has massive technical

Document translation, which was always occurring to some degree throughout Acme, was one of myriad hidden activities that only received attention when there were problems. But now Sanderson recalled just how problem-rich document translation had been during the original plant launch. At that time the process ran at least 10% over budget, was habitually late, and caused delays and quality problems in production.

The combined importance and messiness of the translation process prompted Sanderson to cautiously consider Porter's responsibilities for the expansion. He felt confident that with coaching Porter would be able to get the job done and prevent a repeat of problems in the translation process. Furthermore, Sanderson reasoned that tackling this messy problem could be a great developmental opportunity for Porter.

Porter had been successful in most of his assignments so far. But he had no experience with such a cross-functional administrative process, and had shown a hesitancy to take action when he was in unfamiliar territory. His performance appraisal history showed that he seemed to like certainty and was uncomfortable in new situations.

requirements that must be translated from Japanese documents. The size and complexity of the project are creating errors and delays."

He then worked quickly through the other sections of his A3 template:

- *Current Conditions*: Cost overruns. Delays. Errors. Complexity.
- *Goals/Targets*: Reduce cost by 10%. Reduce problems to manageable rate and simplify processes.
- *Analysis*: Challenge of translating from Japanese to English. Complexity and amount of documents. Problems stemming from multiple vendors.
- *Proposed Countermeasures*: Simplify and improve process performance by choosing one vendor based on competitive bid process.
- *Plan*: Evaluate current vendors. Identify new vendor candidates. Develop bid package, distribute, and choose winning bid.
- *Followup*: Monitor cost to proposal. Review performance at end of one-year contract. Put contract up for bid again if performance goals are not met.

Porter looked it over, pleased, and then took his A3 to Sanderson for approval. His boss was out on the shopfloor, so Porter left the report on his desk.

Sanderson believed that Porter would be able to work his way through the mechanical aspects of the translation problems. His natural people skills also would help him engage a very diverse mix of individuals and groups. However, he would need to stretch himself to learn how to handle more organizational complexity and uncertainty than he had experienced before.

Sanderson knew that assigning this responsibility to Porter meant that he was also assigning responsibility to himself to coach Porter through it.

Whose Problem Is This?

Sanderson returned to find Porter leaving an A3 on his desk. He walked over, picked it up, took a glance at the paper, and looked over to Porter.

"That was quick," Sanderson said.

"Thank you," replied Porter, unsure of Sanderson's intent.

"That wasn't a compliment but an observation. So you've been able to confirm the problem and define a plan of action?" Sanderson asked, handing the A3 back to Porter. "This is your A3, right?"

Porter realized he hadn't signed the report, but resisted the impulse to initial it and hand it right back to Sanderson. It had seemed trivial to him before, but he remembered that every report included the initials of the owner of the A3: *Clear indication of ownership is important so everyone involved can know precisely who is taking responsibility for the problem or proposal.*

Without a word, Porter took the A3 and returned to his desk. He pulled out a file of A3s prepared by other Acme managers. He noticed that each A3 included an initial and date. But more importantly, they seemed to share a common quality. Most were rough, erased, scribbled over as a result of people making many iterative changes. He was beginning to understand: *The A3 owner indicates the draft date because A3s continually evolve and improve in the course of their use. Readers need to know that they are looking at the current version, and can chart the progress of an A3.*

Porter looked up to see Sanderson standing in front of him.

Beginner's Mind

Sanderson appreciated Porter's enthusiastic effort to solve the problem quickly and cost-effectively. Yet he knew that this first zealous rush to own a solution was certain to bar a full investigation of what was going on and prevent a thorough exploration of the best approach to the problem.

He needed to help Porter avoid simply being "right," jumping to a solution, or attaching himself to one course of action. So he focused his work with Porter on coaching his attitude and expectations as much as his method.

Porter needed careful coaching at this stage in his learning process to maintain what some refer to as "a beginner's mind," an openness to many possibilities. Porter needed to look at the document-translation process with an open mind in order to see many possibilities rather than focusing only on a limited set of choices.

"Please take your time," Sanderson encouraged him. "I'm not asking you to neatly fill in all the blanks. The point is to think about the content. Reflect on what the problem really is. Why is it important? How does it tie into what we are trying to accomplish? Don't even worry about the plan of action yet. How could you complete a plan of action when you haven't even confirmed whether there is a problem and, if so, what the problem is?"

Sanderson left. Believing his initial ideas were essentially *right*, Porter initialed the report, added the date, and left it on Sanderson's desk (*see pages 22–23*).

The leader's job is to develop people.

Porter's A3—Rush to a Solution

Is this the issue?

Create Robust Process for Translating Documents

I. Background

"Massive?" How big or important is this problem?

New domestic plant expansion has massive technical requirements that must be translated from Japanese documents to English. The size and complexity of the project are creating errors and delays.

II. Current Conditions

How much? How long? How many?

Cost overruns, delays, and errors due to:

- Sheer volume of documents.
- Multiple and varied vendors (pricing, quality, ease).
- Involvement of various departments and working styles.

III. Goals/Targets

?????

- Simplify and standardize the process.
- Reduce costs by 10%.

Why 10%?

IV. Analysis

What do "challenge" and "complex" mean? What "problems" and what "cause?"

- Challenge of translating from Japanese to English.
- Multiple varied vendors create a complex, nonstandard process.
- Overall improvement can be defined by reduction in cost overruns.

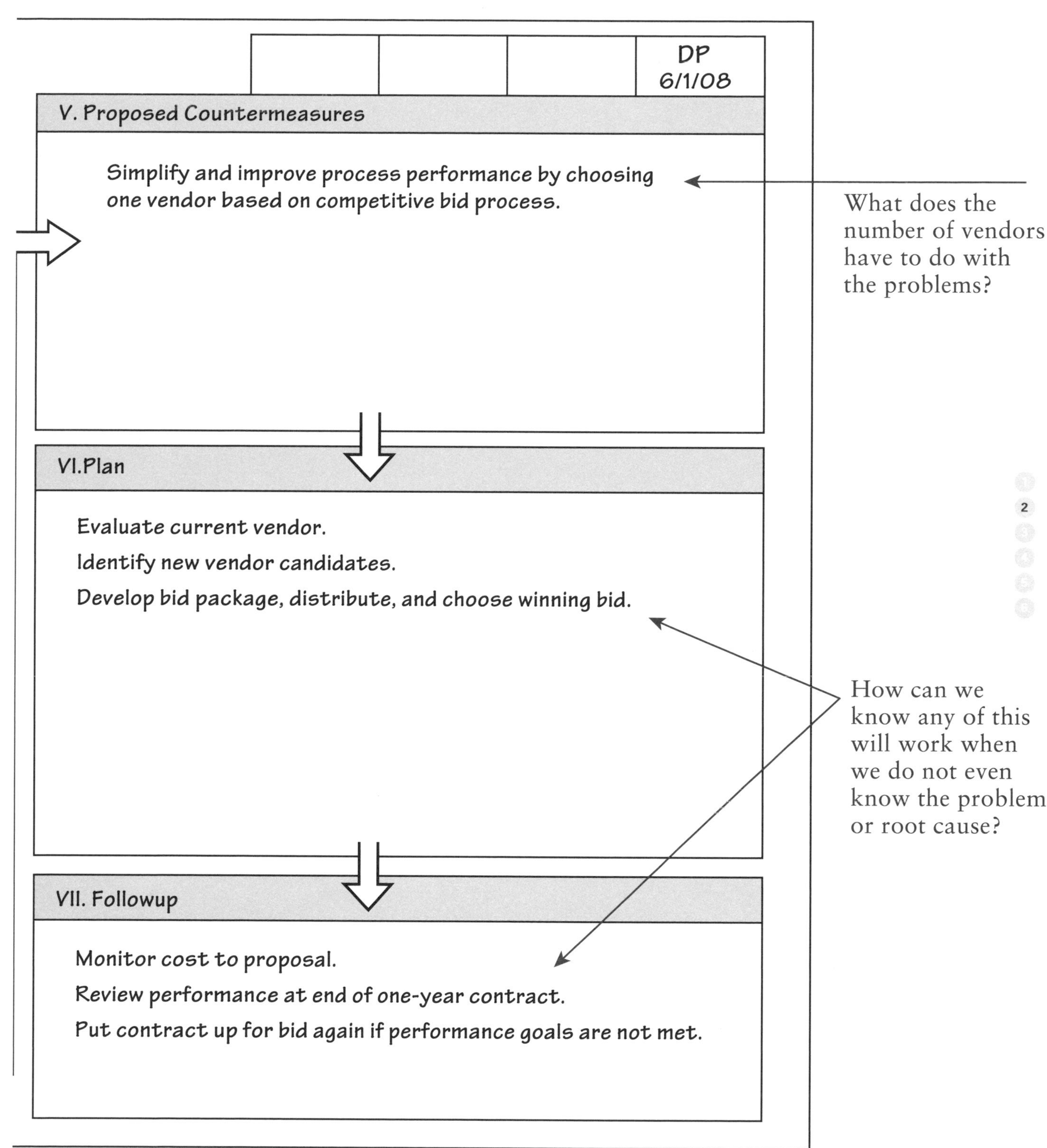
DP
6/1/08
V. Proposed Countermeasures
Simplify and improve process performance by choosing one vendor based on competitive bid process.
VI.Plan
Evaluate current vendor.
Identify new vendor candidates.
Develop bid package, distribute, and choose winning bid.
VII. Followup
Monitor cost to proposal.
Review performance at end of one-year contract.
Put contract up for bid again if performance goals are not met.
What does the number of vendors have to do with the problems?
How can we know any of this will work when we do not even know the problem or root cause?
2

How Do You Really Know What the Problem Is?

Sanderson had studied the "revised" A3 from Porter. "OK, before we talk about the specifics of your proposal, let's talk about the problem. What exactly is the problem you are trying to address?"

"The costs are too high, the process is too slow, and there are too many errors," Porter replied warily, pointing to this information on the paper.

"And how do you know that?" asked Sanderson.

"From talking with Frances in Purchasing and others," answered Porter.

"What else have you discovered?"

"The process is very complex. We have multiple vendors with varying cost and performance."

"Why?"

"Japanese-to-English translation is very difficult. There is a large volume of work to complete in a short amount of time."

Sanderson sat back and replied deliberately, "That's all very general and vague. Do you know how the process actually works? Can you tell me what is causing the problems and delays? What is actually causing the cost overruns?"

"Well, the work gets backed up, and the translators have to work overtime," said Porter.

"So, the delays cause backlogs, which cause overtime. Good. Now we're getting somewhere. So then what causes the delays?"

"Well," Porter said, thinking hard, "I think it's just the sheer volume of work."

"Perhaps," Sanderson said. "Tell me, do you know how the process actually works?"

Questioning Mind

Very neat and tidy; and yet deeply flawed, thought Sanderson as he reviewed Porter's proposal. He had seen this type of thinking many times before: a rush to judgment in order to quickly be right.

The biggest flaw with Porter's initial A3, and the underlying thinking behind it, was that he had jumped to a conclusion about the problem, about what had caused it, and what to do about it. This type of thinking was prevalent among Acme's young managers, and it troubled Sanderson. He had seen too much of it—good people wanting to get work done, jumping to conclusions, and applying poor fixes that are doomed to fail over the long-term.

Sanderson knew that simply showing Porter his error would not necessarily lead him to "get it." He reflected on a key lesson he had discovered: Avoid telling your people exactly what to do. Whenever you tell them what to do you take the responsibility away from them. He understood the essence of leadership is getting individuals to take initiative to continually improve on their own. He could help Porter by getting him to explore the "why" of the situation while making it clear that Porter was the one to work the "how."

That's why his first action had been to get Porter to accept ownership of the problem. Getting him to write his

"Well, the documents originate from our Japanese production shops. They are sent to one of three translators, who perform their work and then send them to the appropriate person in the appropriate shop," said Porter.

"And how do you know this?" Sanderson asked.

"I read through some documents from the initial plant startup," Porter said. "And I based my plans on what I knew and what I had heard around the plant. And I talked with Frances in procurement."

"I see," Sanderson said. "How can you tell how well this is working? What performance criteria are you using?

"I see you've looked at cost," Sanderson continued. "What about quality? Does the vendor with the highest quality have the same lead time as the others?"

"I don't know," replied Porter, surprised that Sanderson seemed to understand the nuances of the overall process as well or better than he did.

"And are some of the vendors easier to work with?" Sanderson asked. "Does that affect the quality of the work? And is the quality of the text translation different than that of the charts and graphs? Are there particular cultural challenges, such as the use of idioms that crop up in particular documents and require special attention? Do all the forms go through the same steps? Do they require different types of translators?"

"I don't know," was all Porter could say repeatedly. He realized that he had filled in all the boxes of his A3 form, but his approach was essentially worthless. He was surprised to find that his boss knew so much about the situation. initials on the A3 was just a first (and largely symbolic) step to encourage Porter to take initiative for the entire process. Sanderson was tempted to go further but stopped himself. He had a clear idea of what he wanted Porter to do, but directing him too much would prevent Porter from thinking for himself and learning the key lesson of *taking ownership*.

Prior to his second conversation with Porter, Sanderson recalibrated his approach. He spent time studying Porter's A3. He walked around the plant, and talked with individuals in his plant and other company plants. He was mindful of finding a way to help Porter find his own answers. He needed to do some research, not to solve the problem himself, but enough to know how to help Porter dig deeper and become a better problem-solver.

Sanderson wanted to help Porter avoid what experienced lean thinkers consider one of the gravest errors: appearing to know something concrete about a situation without having precise, direct knowledge.

He could lead Porter best through influence rather than instruction. This meant getting into the messy details and coaching him through the learning cycles of the work at hand. He avoided the temptation to share preachy homilies about work. He had learned from his Acme experience that the

This attention to detail made it clear to Porter that he needed to go see the nature of the actual problem, rather than applying a quick fix without understanding what had created the problems in the first place.

Porter was beginning to see that the first job when solving the problem was discovering precisely what the problem really was. Writing out a description of what he had been told was insufficient. In order to address a problem, he would need to determine what had created the problem in the first place. Simply producing an A3 wasn't a sign that he had finished his job; in fact, he saw that his work had merely just begun. He needed to go to the gemba.

most effective leaders earned worker loyalty through a careful "operator-out" approach. Leaders earned their stripes by building effective ways of work from the ground-up. They helped individuals see their work, thereby creating opportunities to remove wasteful steps. Helping people create more value on their own represented one of the highest forms of respect. Those individuals who were able to generate this type of constant improvement were the most natural and effective leaders.

Gemba Is More than a Place

Gemba (also spelled "ge*n*ba" with an *n*) is the Japanese term for "actual place," and describes the place where value-creating work happens. While lean practitioners often use the term to describe the shopfloor in manufacturing, gemba describes any setting in which individuals are creating value for a customer. It can refer to office settings, service settings, a hospital ward, or the shopfloor—anywhere that work takes place.

Real improvement only can take place when there is a front-line focus based on direct observation of current conditions where work is done. Toyota calls this principle, *genchi genbutsu shugi*, meaning the "principle of the real place and real thing." For example, standardized work for a worker on a factory floor cannot be created at a desk in the engineering office; it must be defined and revised at the gemba:

> "Of course, data is important at any gemba. But I place the greatest importance on facts or the 'truth.' For example, when a problem occurs, if our identification of the root cause is even slightly incorrect, then our countermeasure also will be completely out of focus. That is why we use the Five Whys repeatedly and thoroughly. And that attitude is the basis of Toyota's scientific method."[2]

In essence, gemba reflects a philosophy of empiricism—go to the gemba to discover the truth.

2. Taiichi Ohno, *Toyota Production System* (Diamond Press, Tokyo, 1980, first published 1978); John Shook translation.

Going to the Gemba

After his meeting with Sanderson, Porter spent the morning poring over the various types of translated documents that were used in the plant. As he looked for patterns and sought ways to apply an overall fix, such as a standard form for all procedures, he was struck by the sheer variety of the forms. There was a tremendous volume of documents with a great deal of technical detail. And the process to handle it all was chaotic.

He was surprised to discover that there was no single person who knew how the entire process worked. Each department handled its own documents independently—and differently. Porter made an effort to find a key person in each area.

After considerable legwork, Porter pulled together a group of people throughout the plant who could help him see the entire process. He visited them individually, gathering facts and getting ideas. But he still needed to learn more about the actual document-translation process.

Porter paid a visit to Acme's Information Technology (IT) Department. In a heavily air-conditioned control room with no windows, Porter found two technicians, Rick and Terry, who maintained the IT system that handled the substantial data transfer that took place between Acme and its headquarters in Japan. Rick and Terry had been handling this responsibility for Acme since the beginning of operations in the United States, so they knew all the problems that had occurred over the years. Whenever a problem occurred with data transfer, whether corrupt files or printing problems, everyone in the plant knew to go to Rick and Terry.

Gemba Mind

Sanderson remembered a slogan he had heard from his first supervisor at Acme: *If the learner hasn't learned, the teacher hasn't taught.* He was trying to teach Porter and others how to learn a specific, dynamic way of thinking that makes employees learn by doing, by understanding the situation through grasping the reality of the gemba. Ideally this meant teaching on the shopfloor, in the office, or at the shipping dock rather than holding formal training meetings.

He needed to use the process of fixing problems as a way of teaching a new way of thinking. (Sanderson had learned that the Japanese mentors who taught him the learner/teacher slogan had previously learned it from their American mentors decades before.)[3]

Sanderson also needed to encourage individuals to articulate and then share their problems. He wanted them to explain how they intended to address them. The A3 format would help by providing a platform to elicit their thoughts about the problem and their approach. And it created a way to communicate back and forth to evolve and deepen understanding.

The methodical nature of the A3 mentoring required Sanderson to be patient in his dealings with Porter—to

3. *Training Within Industry Report*, (Washington, DC: War Manpower Commission, Bureau of Training, 1945).

During the plant startup they were quite involved in the document-translation issue. Not surprisingly, common technical problems that occurred in the data-transfer process showed up in the translated documents as well. One common problem was that technical documents would fail to print properly.

Whenever that happened, everyone screamed for Rick and Terry, who would figure out how to get them printed. Because of this they had many opportunities to view the various translated documents from the various departments. They knew the comings and goings of the documents, the volume, the problems, the users, and their difficulties. For Porter they became a gold mine of information.

For Rick and Terry, the document-translation process was just a side job, but a big headache for them when things went wrong. When all went well, they got no reward; when problems cropped up, they cleaned up the mess.

The duo naturally looked ahead with trepidation to the deluge of new document-translation needs. And they were wary when Porter showed up, but gradually warmed to him, happy to have someone to listen to their problems.

Porter listened to their woes and war stories, frequently pulling the conversation back to document translation. He thanked them for their input, and asked, "Is there anything else you think I need to know?"

"Well, most of the documents involved the Engineering Department," Rick offered.

This confirmed what Porter had learned from Frances' accounting records and worked into a pie chart. Engineering had the greatest volume of documents to be translated.

Documents by Department

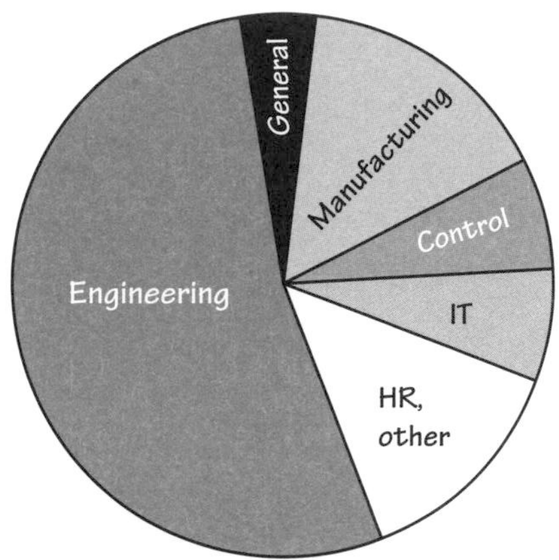

2

"Yes, but most of the headaches come from manufacturing operations," Terry added.

Porter described the idea he and Frances had developed, that of putting the process up for competitive bid and choosing the one best vendor.

"Sure. And we know the one to choose," said Rick, with Terry agreeing.

Porter took furious notes as Rick and Terry recommended the vendor that caused them the fewest headaches. After thanking them again for their help, Porter gathered up the forms and went to confer with Sanderson about what he had discovered, excited about his solution of a competitive bid to choose one vendor.

"I'm glad to see you've got a better handle on the overall process," Sanderson replied. "What about the actual work?"

a point. Like supervisors everywhere, he also felt the pressure of broader organizational goals he needed to achieve. His own A3 addressing overall plant quality and shipping delays, of which translation-related defects were but one factor, reflected the urgency of being successful with this A3 management process.

Indeed, his timeline reflected these interconnected demands. Much effort had gone into putting it together and the result was a time-driven plan with the activities and objectives of numerous organizations intertwined, mutually dependent on the others to keep pace by performing and delivering their piece of the puzzle.

What Is a Problem?

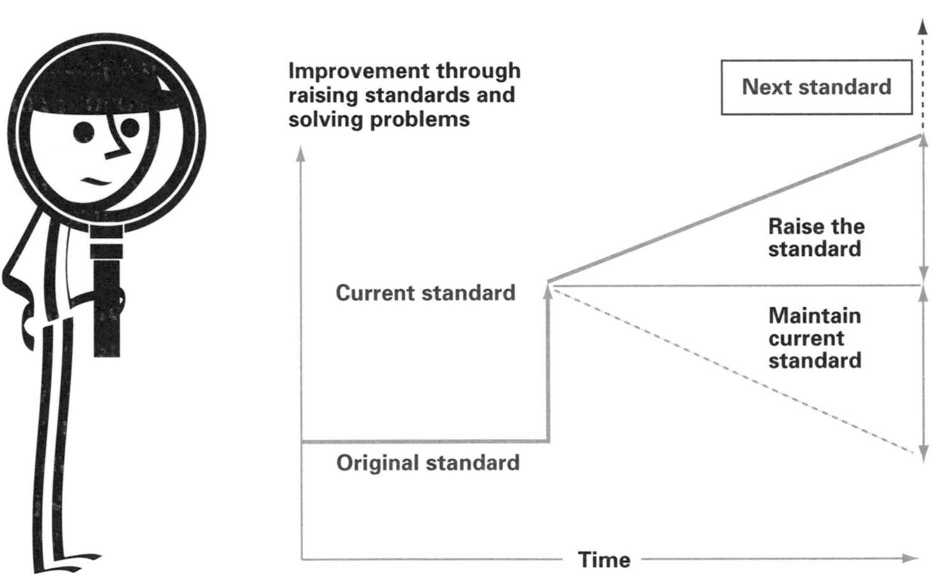

A problem is any performance other than desired performance at any given time.

"The actual work?" Porter asked.

"Yes, the actual translation work. Do you know why the performance of the three vendors varies so much?"

"No. I could hazard some guesses. But does it really matter?"

Sanderson looked at him, "You want to understand the problem, right?"

"Got it—back to the gemba."

Porter took his investigation to the translation vendors. He discovered that the translators were just as frustrated as anyone else. The challenges they faced were significant. Many of the Japanese documents they received were illegible. They often spent more time getting the originals into readable form than doing the actual translation.

The documents included many drawings and charts that were difficult to translate and recreate faithfully. And there were many idioms, colloquialisms, and abbreviations unique to the company and that varied from jobsite to jobsite, and even job to job.

He found that there were three basic types of documents to be translated:

1. Office documents, such as policies, procedures, and general training materials, that could be translated by a general translator.
2. Technical engineering documents that required an engineering translator.
3. Job instructions: Descriptive documents detailing standard work; these were best done by translators who were close to the gemba.

Sanderson was the expansion launch project manager, but there were many functions and departments over which he had no direct control. He needed to get these groups to march forward together, working mostly separately but still in sync. In particular, product development and sales and marketing were completely out of his oversight or easy sphere of influence; they were dependent on him delivering the production and logistical capability to deliver the right product with the desired quality to the customer on time.

Sanderson had much work ahead.

Documents by Type

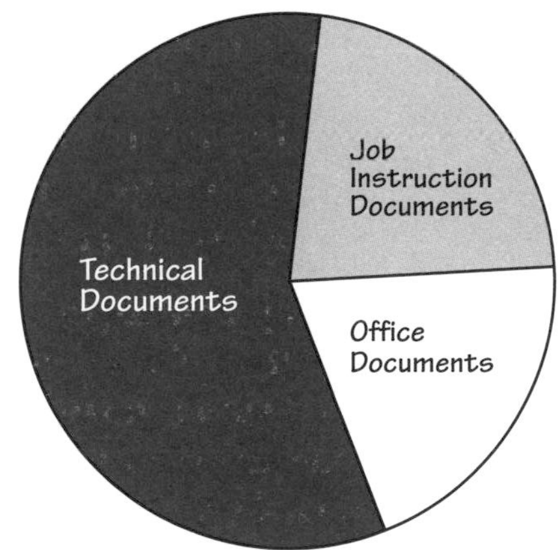

What's the Problem?

Or, first, what is a problem? Organizations spend enormous amounts of time and energy debating, exploring, and trying solutions—yet, how often is it clearly asked and answered, *"Just what problem are we are trying to solve?"*

Simply clarifying what we mean when we say "problem" can be powerful. A problem is something that presents itself as a barrier to the organization achieving its goals (a presenting problem or the issue that is presenting itself to you) and in some way relates to the way the work is designed or being done (a problem in the work). To solve the presenting problem or the problem in the work it is helpful to see the relationship between problem-solving and improvement and between improvement and standardized work.

The anatomy of problems and improvement:

Presenting problems and problems in the work: A presenting problem is the problem immediately facing you, an actual pain felt by the organization, or a gap between current and desired conditions, such as reduced profits, increased cost, diminished sales, a safety hazard, etc. A problem in the work is any deviation from the *standard way of doing things* or the regular routine or "kata." A "kata" typically refers to fundamental martial-arts movements, but can refer to any basic form, routine, or pattern of behavior. Recognizable patterns of behavior and clear expectations make it easy to recognize abnormalities (problems) and also serve as a basis for improvement, setting and attaining higher standards.

Problems and improvement: Whether trying to maintain current levels of performance or aiming for new and higher levels, the identification of standards is requisite. As shown in the illustration on page 30, knowledge of the gap between current and desired levels of performance sets the stage for performance improvement.

Improvement and standardized work: The central role of standardized work in improvement is one of the most important and underutilized aspects of TPS outside of Toyota. A common misperception of standardization is that it is regimentation or command and control. Not so. The true value of standard work is to serve as the basis for experimentation. Standards are set—as bases of comparison—and are used as baselines for improvement. As long as current standards are as they are, there should be no deviation. However, if someone has a better idea for how to perform his or her own work, that idea is proposed, approved, tried, evaluated against the current standard, and rewarded. Far from regimenting individual work into robotic chores, standardized work can enable individual innovation at every level of the organization. As with traditional Japanese arts where the learner first masters the basic form of the "kata," mastery of fundamentals of standardized work results in individual innovation being enabled and encouraged.

Understanding any problem is the first step to improvement and, theoretically, resolving it.[4] Conceptual agreement on what a problem is in general makes it easy to clarify what the problem is in a specific situation. As Charles "Boss" Kettering was known to say, "A problem well stated is a problem half-solved."[5]

4. See page 65 for a discussion of "Countermeasures vs. Solutions."
5. Attributed to Charles F. Kettering (1876-1958).

Porter sighed. The more he learned about the problem, the more challenging it became. Prior to going to the gemba, he was armed with some data, hearsay, and ideas derived from his own experiences. Now that he had gone to the gemba, he was certain he could develop a better plan. Even though he wasn't sure how to fix this whole mess or fully understand why things were so messy, he did, for the first time, feel like he was beginning to see the mess.

Porter thought, *Maybe this is what progress feels like*. Once more he sat at his desk to address the problem. He had gone to the gemba and learned from what he saw. He produced a revised A3 titled, "Deliver perfect translations," which captured what he had learned from his investigation, no more, filling in only the *Background* and *Current Conditions* sections *(see page 34)*.

2

Key Questions

- Who is responsible for this issue? Who owns the process for addressing the problem (or realizing the opportunity or managing the project)?
- What is the business context? How did you decide to tackle this problem?
- What do you actually know and how do you know it?
- Have you gathered and verified facts—not just data and anecdotes—to clearly understand the current state?
- Have you engaged other people?
- What is the problem? Can you clearly and succinctly define the "presenting problem"—the actual business issue that is being felt?
- Have you gone to the gemba?

Porter's First Revised A3

Is this the right title?

Deliver Perfect Translations

I. Background

Acme plant to double capacity!

→ Much document translation required!

- Poor English translations of Japanese documents caused many problems at original plant startup.
- Expansion plans call for aggressive launch timeline and cost reduction.

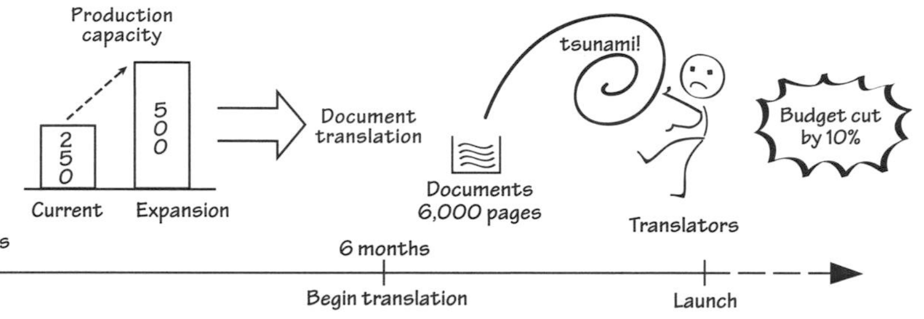

→ Document translation problems could impede plant launch!

II. Current Conditions

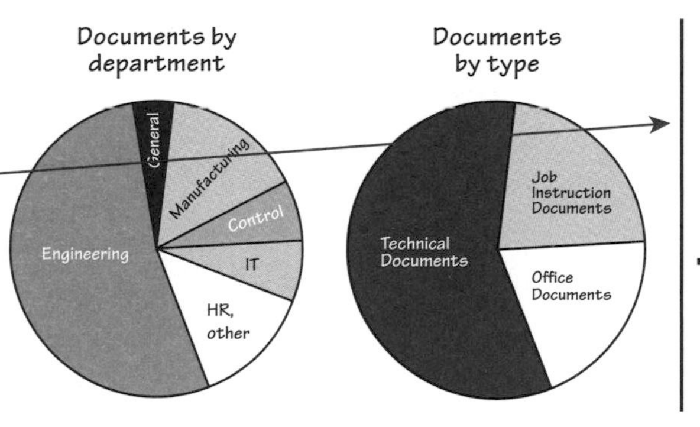

Problems in document translation at time of initial plant launch:

Cost = High

Delivery = Highly variable

Quality = Many errors!

→ Problems in document translation process have not been corrected!

How high?

How variable?

How many errors?

succinct → fewer words

timeline as a visual

data adds more definition + clarity

focusing on current conditions, not jumping ahead

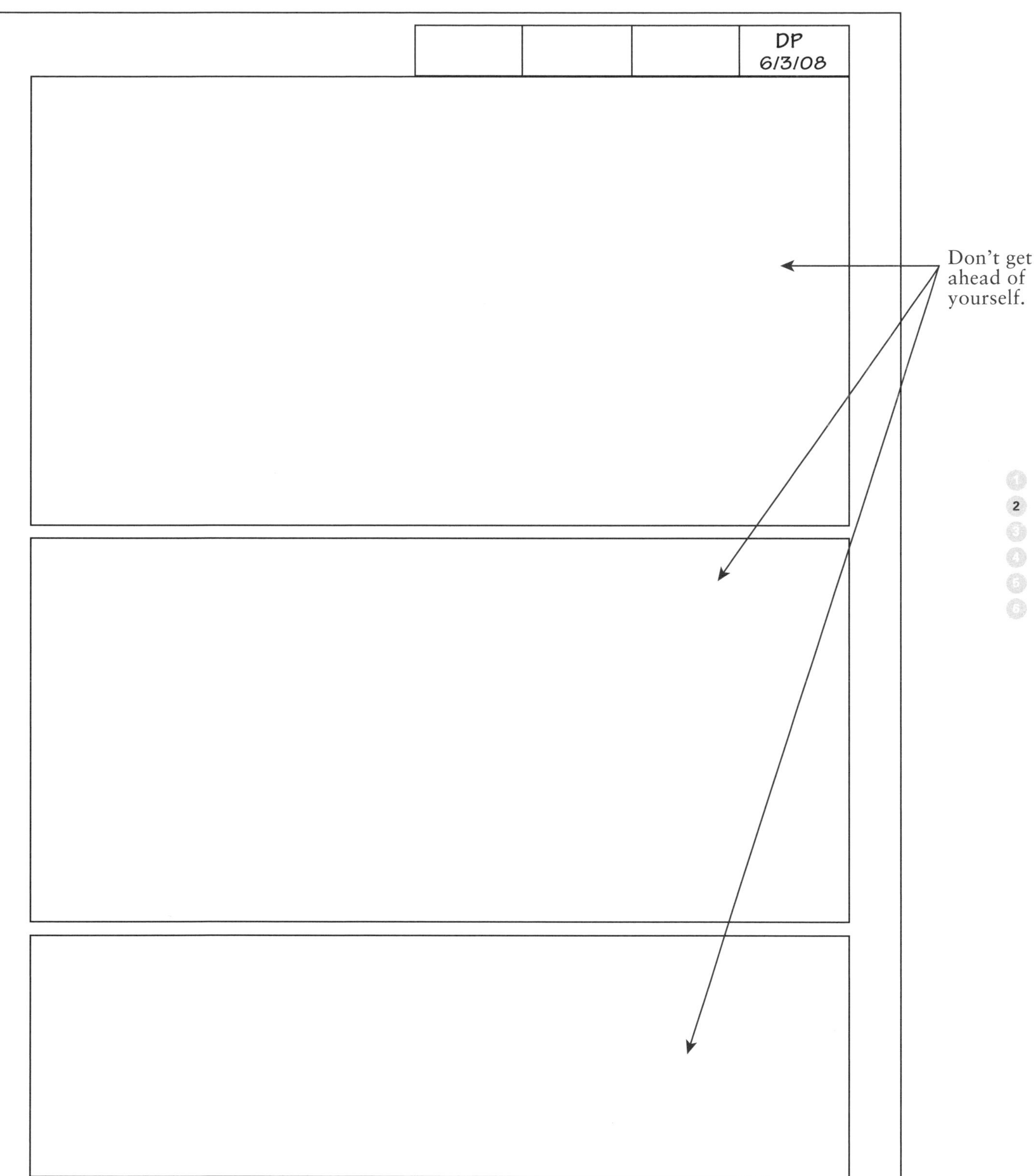
DP
6/3/08
Don't get ahead of yourself.

Chapter 3
Goals and Analysis—Finding the Root Cause

Initially Porter seeks a single, quick *solution* to the document-translation problem. But he learns through this experience that he must get to the root cause of the problem. After some missteps, he begins a more rigorous root-cause examination of how the process produces errors and defects. He learns, through Sanderson's mentoring, how to use the Five Whys technique to investigate until he discovers the true point of cause and then to present these facts in a manner that invites conversation and action.

Sanderson, meanwhile, continues to teach and mentor Porter by setting the stage for him to learn and take initiative; at the same time Sanderson seeks to hasten this process in light of myriad problems he faces in his own role. Moreover, Sanderson works to present the tools and techniques in a manner that spells out the underlying system, so that every activity becomes a learning activity. If Porter can learn how to get at the why behind the why, then he could develop into a leader himself.

What Is the Problem?

As Sanderson studied Porter's most recent A3, Porter proudly pointed out how he had tracked and documented all the activities that might affect the translation process, including a folder of charts and spreadsheets to illustrate his points. He was particularly excited about his revised A3, which indicated his intent to redesign and establish standardized work for all translation activities.

"The problem is we have no standardized work. I think that we would generate some quick and very powerful benefits if we do a better job of standardizing how the translators process their documents," Porter told Sanderson. "What's happening right now is that the variety of requirements is creating delays, confusion, and variation in processing time. Standard templates would solve a lot of these problems."

To Porter's relief, Sanderson seemed to be nodding in agreement as he reviewed the document. He paused before speaking. "Remember that an A3 isn't just a collection of facts and data. It should tell a story, a problem-solving story. It should bring the facts and data to life, and point toward a way to a better future state.

"This A3 does a better job of sharing data that you've gathered at the gemba," he said to Porter. "You've also concluded that eliminating variance from the overall process will pay off. But how do you know that this problem is the real problem?"

Porter was puzzled. Hadn't he just done that? More than puzzled, he began to feel a bit deflated as he replied, "Isn't the problem that we have no standardized work?"

Don't Be a Hero

Sanderson was torn. He was pleased that Porter had gone to the gemba and taken initiative to devise his own proposal for addressing the situation. And yet, Porter's fast approach was still entirely insufficient.

A quick and easy fix that reduced costs might well simplify the process, but it could just as easily generate waste in many other linked areas and might not even solve the real problems—whatever they were. And that was the problem: Porter hadn't really defined the problem or problems.

He had identified an overall condition of complexity—which would benefit from clearer and commonly understood standard work. Yet Porter still seemed motivated to frame his problem in a grand manner that lent itself to a dramatic and over-arching *solution.*

Sanderson knew that "solving" a perceived problem based on gut instincts was a tempting path, especially for someone like Porter who was beginning to take some ownership of this process. It's hard for anyone to resist fixing something *now.* Sanderson needed to douse this heroic urge without undermining Porter's progress and spirit.

Sanderson recognized this encounter as part of a broader company problem,

Sanderson took the A3 report, moved behind Porter's desk, and held it before them so each was seeing it from the same perspective. He asked Porter to go back to the A3 form and review the purpose of the *Goals/Targets* and *Analysis* sections. "You need to discern which problems and facts are actually causing pain to the organization. And then, for each of those problems, you need to identify its root cause.

"I am still confused about the exact nature of the problems and the cause of the problems," Sanderson continued. "Be careful to avoid confusion among symptoms, root causes, and solutions. It's not clear to me which pieces of data you've provided point to the root problem we need to deal with—some support your solution and others, while accurate, tell us about an outcome or symptom.

"What real 'pain' is the organization feeling? Try organizing your findings with a simple question: 'What keeps us from reaching what we want to achieve, our future state, our target condition?'"

"Well, the first pain the organization is feeling is the cost overages," began Porter, recalling with some irritation how he thought his first A3 had pointedly addressed this perceived problem.

"Okay," Sanderson acknowledged, "and what about the pain felt by the customers of this process? What pain does this process cause for the engineers and others who need the translated documents, the customers of the process? Is cost their biggest concern?"

"Shouldn't cost be a concern for everyone?"

"Cost is always a concern. But is it the biggest concern in this case? Have you asked the engineers and others what their biggest concerns are? The and one that he had seen in most every organization everywhere: a stubborn "firefighting mentality." Even within Acme, which had provided extensive lean training, senior leaders continued to unwittingly create and then honor heroes. These individuals successfully responded to crises with dramatic solutions—yet did little to prevent these crises from occurring in the first place.

Sanderson wanted Porter to see the flaws in this heroic aspiration, and guide him on a different course. He shared the story of the baseball shortstop who was acclaimed for always making great athletic plays. His coach then pointed out that he was often out of position to begin with.

Perhaps worse, Porter was still grasping at improvement tools as hammers looking for nails. He had unknowingly worked back from a standardized work solution to see a standardized work problem. Given Porter's past operations experience and training with lean, it wasn't unusual that he'd grab at something with which he was familiar, in this case standardized work.

This was another common problem at Acme. With a full suite of lean tools in place at Acme, many individuals had gotten the wrong idea that the purpose of the tool is the tool itself. To counter this tendency, Sanderson and other members of the Acme

translated documents are required to support the launch of new production, right? Exactly how will problems with translated documents affect the launch?"

Porter thought about this, and said, "I know they are concerned about timeliness and waiting on needed documents. Late documents create all types of problems."

"What else?" asked Sanderson.

"Well," Porter continued, "even when the documents arrive on time, if there are errors in the translation, production problems can result. One document during the plant startup contained incorrectly translated safety procedures, which almost caused a serious accident."

"Good, so you've just covered cost, delivery, and quality; those are real business problems that cause real pain to the organization," Sanderson acknowledged. "Now do you know what causes each of those problems?"

"Well, the cost issue can be addressed by my proposal to institute a competitive bid process ...," started Porter.

Sanderson interrupted him, "That's not what I asked. Why do we have cost overages? What causes them?"

As Porter began to explain that the cause is variation in the cost of the different vendors, he could anticipate Sanderson's next question.

"So, why is there such variation in cost?"

Porter realized he didn't know the answer to the question. He waited for his boss to continue.

"Variation must mean that sometimes costs are lower than other times. Yes? And why is it that senior management team watched for this kind of tail-wagging-the-dog thinking and took steps to provide just-in-time coaching in root-cause analysis.

Sanderson had to be careful, though, because he didn't want to dampen Porter's pride of achievement; quite the contrary. He wanted to keep his enthusiasm up, in a manner that fostered a more productive focus. He wanted to create a company of problem-solvers whose heroism would be reflected by the fact that "crises" rarely occurred in the first place. (If the shortstop positioned himself properly, he wouldn't be forced to make all those great athletic plays on a regular basis.) The patient character of farmers was more descriptive of this community of problem-solvers than hunters or superheroes.

So Sanderson maintained his focus on pushing Porter to probe deeper, both with identifying and then analyzing problems. Developing individuals who looked deeply to understand the problems at hand through root-cause analysis would gradually lessen the need for heroes. It would set the stage for a broader spirit of continuous learning. And once problems were thoroughly understood, potential solutions would begin to reveal themselves.

sometimes the work can be done at lower cost than other times? How much variation is there? What actually constitutes the cost, anyway?"

Porter answered, "To the best of my knowledge, the budget overruns were largely caused by overtime and expediting charges. So most of the cost problems were caused by delivery issues."

"Lead time?" Sanderson asked.

"Yes, exactly," Porter confirmed.

"And what causes the lead-time issues?"

"Well," Porter replied thoughtfully, "I think there is natural variation in the work itself. That is, some translators work faster than others and some translations can be done faster than others."

Sanderson could see that Porter did not yet have a handle on the nature of the real problems, much less a grasp of the root causes.

Therefore, Sanderson saw that his immediate challenge was simply to get Porter to *realize* that he didn't know these things and to be open to—and even excited about—learning a new path of discovery. He knew that this was a lesson that was not easy to learn, recalling his own mentor's words: "Don't be afraid to admit when you don't know—'I don't know' is a fine answer."

Breaking Down the Problem

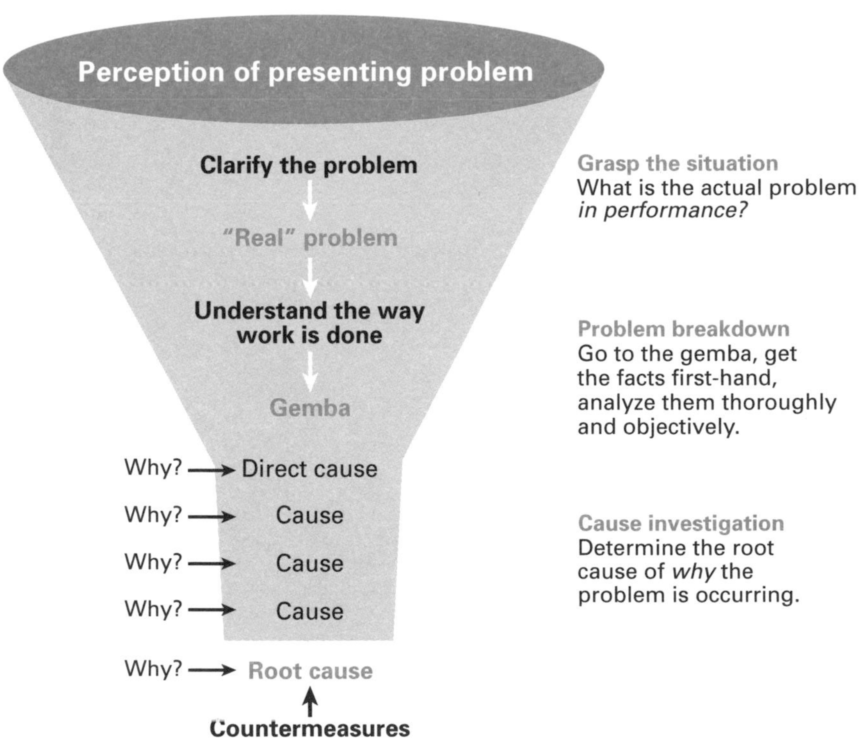

"That is interesting." Sanderson replied, finally getting to the point he wanted Porter to see. "Can you find any patterns in the amount of time required to translate different kinds of documents by different translators? What are the factors in getting documents through the process and into the hands of the people who need them?"

Porter realized he didn't know nearly enough about the process to answer those questions. But Sanderson's insistence on pinpointing the exact factors that stood between current state and the ideal had helped frame the process in a way that made powerful sense to him.

"Of course, the target condition, the real goal," thought Porter. He was upset that he'd become so infatuated with facts about the gemba and the attractiveness of standard work as a solution that he had lost sight of the real problems affecting Acme. He thought back to the targets discussed when he was assigned the translation A3—errors, delivery time, cost, and ease of process. "OK," he thought, "what's the gap between these targets and the conditions I've observed? That's where the problems are. Then I've just got to find the reasons that each of those problems are there."

The scientific mind does not so much provide the right answers as ask the right questions.[1]

—Claude Lévi-Strauss

1. Claude Lévi-Strauss, anthropologist.

Lost in Translation

Porter sat at his desk and combed through the documents he had prepared for his A3. He compared the target with the current conditions, and realized that many of his findings, charts, and spreadsheets were irrelevant.

He needed to develop a clearer understanding of the problem in order to organize his thinking and his learning. And in this case the key beacon that needed to shape his understanding was "the gap" between the current and target state.

Porter remembered the first A3 that he had ever written. The problem had, in fact, been easy to solve. There had been a single root cause that was uncovered through a simple problem-saving exercise. A grinding machine had been generating excess scrap. Interestingly, the machine had been in operation for almost three years with no problem. It hadn't been that hard to track down what changed (why was it generating scrap now when it was fine for three years) and what caused it. Looking back, he remembered the rich data he had at his fingertips and recognized how this made everything seem so straightforward.

Some problems, however, defied a clear analysis and clean solution. But getting rid of some of the noise in his earlier findings would be a good start. For the document-translation problem, it didn't matter how many reams of paper were used; paper was not a contributor to quality or delivery problems. The same was true of his chart tracking problems with servers in the IT department; Rick and Terry made sure any problems that occurred were quickly addressed.

Framing for Understanding

Sanderson was sympathetic with Porter's struggle. He, too, had been in engineering prior to his current position, and his early experience led him to see the A3 process as a straightforward, problem-solving tool.

A3s in engineering settings dealt with straightforward problems and clear solutions found through a deductive investigative process. Clearly this was a large reason why Porter (like Sanderson before him) was so certain that he had found such an immediate and obvious solution.

But Porter's current translation problem —like most problems in nonmanufacturing operations—was much messier than the engineering problems he had encountered previously. He was finding it extremely difficult to even find out exactly what was going on (there was woefully little data, in great contrast with what he had become accustomed to in engineering), to identify the problems, and to determine what his "future state" should even look like, much less how to get there. Sanderson was ready for this wall of reality to hit Porter.

Sanderson needed to help Porter discover the key principles that will help inform his investigative process, even when the clues are not so clear.

Everyone he talked to seemed to have "ideas" or opinions and many reams of data, but no one seemed to have any facts. What was really wrong with the process that had been used during the initial start of operations? What were the goals for the new process?

"To solve the problem you'll need to break it down so you can identify *why* the problem is there, what causes it," Sanderson explained. "Those causes will be the targets of your countermeasures."

Porter knew what he needed to do. "I should analyze the problem more deeply, identify the gaps and look for reasons why the gaps exist, why the problems occur," he said. Porter renewed his investigation, determined to dig deeper into the causes for the problems.

Before he could design a new system, Porter would need to clarify two things: where things currently stand, and where they need to go.

The bigger issue here was the need to show Porter how he could solve this problem himself, and how he could then use the same problem-solving skills for the next problem he encountered. And the next and the next.

Breaking Down Porter's Problem

One thread: Errors due to language problems in original Japanese documents

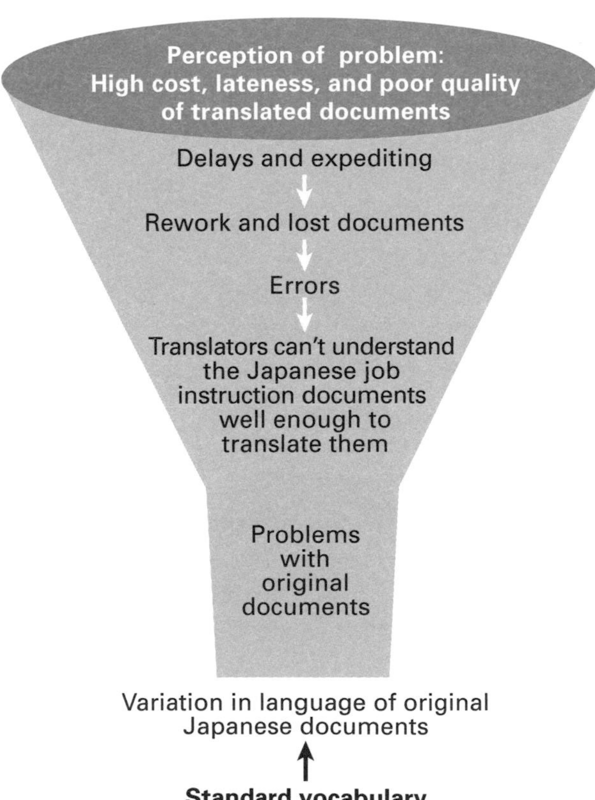

Digging Deeper

Once again Porter revised his A3, documenting what he believed were the problems. This time he defined "problems" as instances where gaps existed between the current conditions and the goal. By now he had lost count of how many times he had revised the original A3. He felt frustrated that creating something so seemingly simple was so difficult and taking so long. But he had learned some valuable lessons.

For example, Porter now recognized that he should not jump to a solution and should spend more time asking questions about how the work was handled. He followed specific documents through every step in the translation process to observe what happened. He avoided quick conclusions, seeking instead to pursue his inquiry into why things were occurring.

Now Porter thought about those conversations as he considered the *Goals/Targets* on his A3 and the gap analysis that would, he hoped, eventually help him to reach the goal.

In the *Goals/Targets* section of the A3, Porter wrote out what he considered to be reasonable targets based on initial conversations with Sanderson, his many observations at the gemba, and the ongoing feedback from those actually touching the process. He believed his goals were aggressive but attainable:

- *Cost*: Cut translation costs by 10%.
- *Quality*: Zero defects.
- *Delivery*: 100% on-time for documents needed at startup.
- *Stakeholder satisfaction* (improve the process): Problems visible, communications clear, and all stakeholders have a voice in improvements.

Why Ask Why?

Porter's progress was encouraging to Sanderson. He was developing an ability to use close observation of the work itself as a lens through which he did more of his thinking, inquiry, and planning.

And yet Sanderson needed to prevent this small gain from turning, ironically, into a setback. For Porter would find real improvement to be limited over the long-term by the very tools that helped him achieve short-term gains.

Over years of practice, Sanderson had learned that lean management employs a set of techniques that together form a system. Each tool in isolation will only take someone so far. Used together they constitute a business system to achieve specific business objectives.

So a little understanding at this stage might in fact be dangerous. Pride with mastering the small steps could reduce the urgency, distract Porter, and keep him from understanding the larger lean philosophy and its ability to impact Acme. The Five Whys approach (*see sidebar on page 47*) helps to push for ever more understanding.

He needed to help Porter to work problems down to the level at which they need to be addressed. It's not always going to be five questions in the Five Whys, and he wanted to lead Porter to this understanding. There are times where one gets to the root cause in two questions, and other

His *Analysis* was more specific than what he initially provided to Sanderson, and, he *thought*, similarly based on detailed observations:

- *Cost*: Huge variation depending on the vendor.
- *Quality*: Translators don't pay attention to the quality of their work.
- *Delivery*: Translators have no regard for deadlines.
- *Stakeholder satisfaction* (improve the process): The problems upset everyone and feed resentment, fixing the problems will make everyone happier, and make subsequent work progress more smoothly.

Porter walked over to Sanderson. He handed over the A3, and then took a seat opposite Sanderson.

Sanderson asked him, "Why don't the employees involved in the expansion have the translated documents when they need them?"

"Well, it's right there," said Porter, pointing to the delivery analysis.

"Yeah, I see, but try answering the question I just asked you from the customer's perspective. What would the engineer who is waiting for a translation say?"

"OK, well, some wiseguys would say they can't get their printer to print the documents on time."

"Good. And why can't they get the printer to print the documents on time?"

"What is this, 20 questions?"

"No, just five," replied Sanderson, "as in Five Whys. Keep asking 'why'—maybe five or more times—until you uncover the root cause. But let's not get ahead of ourselves."

occasions where it takes more time. And as Sanderson found out, there are times when the back-and-forth process of asking questions of others can, to the uninitiated, just irritate colleagues. Porter and others at Acme needed to progress at their own pace of lean understanding.

During his time at headquarters operations in Japan, Sanderson had learned that it was taboo for an individual to argue for a solution to a problem they didn't actually know about (a fact which Five Whys would reveal). Similarly taboo was sloppiness in any form, especially in thinking. He was pleased to see Porter learning this on his own.

What Is Five Whys?

Critical to successful implementation of the Toyota Production System is a simple tool commonly referred to as "Five Whys," which is the practice of asking "why" repeatedly whenever a problem is encountered in order to get beyond the obvious symptoms so as to discover the root cause.

In explaining why this practice provides the scientific basis of the Toyota system, Taiichi Ohno said: "To tell the truth, the Toyota Production System has been built on the practice and evolution of this scientific approach. By asking 'why?' five times and answering it each time, we can get to the real cause of the problem, which is often hidden behind more obvious symptoms."[2]

Ohno provides a specific example of Five Whys at work. When confronted with a machine that stopped working, the repeated question uncovered the following cycle of discovery:

1. Why did the machine stop?
   There was an overload and the fuse blew.
2. Why was there an overload?
   The bearing was not sufficiently lubricated.
3. Why was it not lubricated?
   The lubrication pump was not pumping sufficiently.
4. Why was it not pumping sufficiently?
   The shaft of the pump was worn and rattling.
5. Why was the shaft worn out?
   There was no strainer attached and metal scraps got in.

Making this logical sequence clear and explicit enables individuals and teams to concentrate on important matters and to discuss them in productive terms.

Why ask "why?" Ohno would state that who, what, when, where, and how are certainly important, but why supercedes all. In fact, Ohno writes, "Five 'Whys' equal one 'How.'"[3] Effective exploration of the Five Whys can prevent the waste of debating the *five whos*. His message was to never jump to solutions and to keep activities focused to deliver both learning and results. Why save your brainstorming creativity for solutions that may solve the wrong problem? First brainstorm the cause of the problem.

2. Taiicho Ohno, *Toyota Production System: Beyond Large-Scale Production* (New York: Productivity Press, 1988).
3. Ibid.

"OK, aside from the occasional IT system problems that Rick and Terry take care of, a deeper problem is the fact that the translated documents don't get into the system on time," Porter said.

"And why don't they get in the system on time?"

"Because the translators take too long to complete them?"

Sanderson smiled, "And why is that happening?"

"Because the translators work at different paces, partially because of the different kinds of work they do as well as where documents originate," Porter said, pointing to a series of diagrams. "Actually, some documents arrive on time or even early but the material just sits in someone's out-basket while another translator sits with no work to do."

Porter's Problem Breakdown

Sanderson's latest conversation with Porter encouraged him to dig more deeply into what he perceived were the problems:

- Why do errors occur? What kind of errors, and on what kind of documents?

- Why are documents not 100% on time? What percentage are late? How late?
- Why do documents get stuck in the process, or even lost? How many get lost? What happens when they get lost? Are there any patterns?

Lost in Translation—Lost

Never lost
Lost and never found
Lost and found
Just stuck

The Problem beneath the Problem

On his gemba visits Porter had discovered, to his surprise, that not only were there different levels of translating skill among the translators, there were also different types of translators. Some were skilled at understanding technical language, while others were more skilled at nuances of Japanese-American translations, and others were proficient at understanding unique technical colloquialisms. This situation caused much of the inconsistency he had found, and now he was beginning to see how it related to delivery times.

"OK, why are some translators late and having trouble keeping up while there are times when others have nothing to do?" asked Sanderson.

"Well, even though they work at very different rates, we just dump it all out there at once on everybody," exclaimed Porter. "I guess it's because we haven't tried to balance their workloads and schedules—by assigning it based on the kinds of translation work they're doing and their skill levels."

"Good," Sanderson replied encouragingly. "But, be sure to keep problem and countermeasure separate. Yes, the assignment of work is our responsibility and we need to be cognizant of the workers in the system when we analyze workloads and develop schedules. But, even there, you left out a step. Can you see what that is?

"Well," Porter responded, "I can't imagine how else we can deal with the different working pace of the translators."

Gemba Discovery

As Porter compiled and analyzed data on the problems associated with each type of document translated at Acme, he was surprised—and pleased—to see a clear trend emerging. Understanding the characteristics of each document type would help him address the quality (error generation) and delivery (lead time) problems that were occurring, and subsequently, costs associated with them:

- Although technical engineering documents were nearly half of the volume of documents translated, they had proportionally few delivery or quality problems.
- Office documents generated delivery and quality problems proportional to their volume.
- Job instructions, critical to the successful launch of the expansion, accounted for quality and delivery problems highly disproportional to their volume.

Porter's bar chart helped him focus more analysis and attention on the right area—errors in translating job instructions (*see page 50*).

As Sanderson smiled at him, Porter smacked his forehead with his open hand, "Of course!"

"Exactly," said Sanderson, completing Porter's thought. "The question is not, 'How can I fix this?' but 'Why do the translators work at such different rates?'"

"Got it," Porter replied, but then hesitated. "But what can I possibly do about the fact that translators work at different rates? Isn't it natural that there would be substantial variation in that kind of work?"

"Yes, that could be the case. But we don't know that for sure, do we? At this point, we don't know what countermeasures may be possible."

"That's why I need to go back to the gemba, right?" said Porter, laughing as he completed Sanderson's thought.

"Keep asking yourself 'Why?' even when you think you've uncovered the problem," said Sanderson. "That's the true purpose of using the Five Whys. The object is not to ask five times, but to drive your thinking to the root cause, whether this means asking why two times or 10. For complex problems you'll also need to pull in the various problem-solving tools you've learned in industrial engineering. You know, Pareto charts, fishbone diagrams, whatever will help. Some of those may apply to the translation issue. Just start digging in. When you need help, I'll be here."

**Lost in Translation—
Translation Problems**

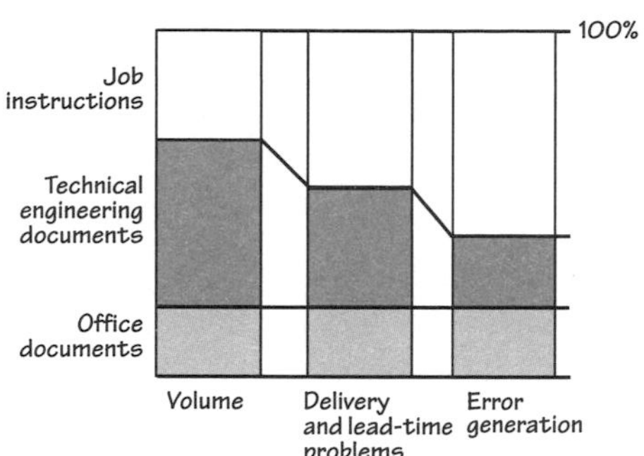

Sanderson was pleased that Porter's revised *Analysis* had the same items as before, but with a completely different, deeper understanding of the presenting problems and their underlying causes:

- *Cost*: Overages from expediting and overtime due to lateness of documents.
- *Delivery*: Documents often late due to both rework and them getting lost somewhere in the system.
- *Quality*: There was much rework and many errors due largely to difficulties with original Japanese documents, especially job instruction documents.
- *Stakeholder satisfaction* (improve the process): The problems upset everyone and feed resentment.

Cost issues were purely related to either delivery or quality problems. Delivery problems broke down into two basic issues: they were late either because of extensive rework or due to simply getting lost somewhere in the system. Porter had pored over the data to break down these two problems, eventually making important discoveries: There was no relation between the type of document and the likelihood of it getting lost, so whatever causes documents to go missing is something that is common among all documents. However, the data and problem breakdown told a different story when it came to rework: some types of documents entailed a much greater amount of rework to produce a quality translation—job instructions.

This discovery led Porter to state the problem differently to Sanderson, which then led him to a surprising realization. When he framed the problem as "Low first-time quality of job instruction translations," it became clear that the cause wasn't that the translators weren't qualified or capable. Rather, the cause was that it was very difficult to produce a quality description of how a job is done without seeing the actual work, and virtually impossible with the rough state of the written descriptions of the original Japanese documents.

Whose Fault?

Porter's investigation and tracking of the issues back through hypothesis and analysis trees uncovered a problem that was both surprising and highly perplexing (*see diagrams on pages 53 and 54*). It turned out the problem of variation in the work of the translators—which he had expected and was eager to tackle—was largely caused by the Acme internal people who generated the original documents, the very "customers" of the process that Porter was trying to please.

Porter talked to Rick and Terry, who recommended that he talk with Ana in Engineering. She coordinated the cataloging of general technical documents, translated and otherwise. "Well, sure the translators are frustrated with the different terminology that we use internally," she said. "It's always been a little frustrating to me, too. Although, honestly, I wonder who causes more problems, the translators or our own engineers. From what you are suggesting, we are our own worst enemy.

"This is similar to a quality problem we had with a component vendor last year. We dispatched a whole team of quality technicians to help them, when the root cause of the problem turned out to be with our original design. I guess we should always look inside first, and turn our attention to suppliers later."

Porter's investigation revealed that errors in the documents led to rework that led to delivery problems. Furthermore, the great majority of the errors were caused by lack of clarity in the original document creation. The result was a messy back and forth between the translators and the Acme

Good People, Poor Systems

It took Sanderson many years to accept that many of the so-called "problem people" in his plant were of his own doing. Occasionally there truly was a bad egg, but most issues for which he and others previously had wanted to point an accusatory finger—safety, quality, delays, waste in all forms—ultimately could be traced back to underperforming processes that were owned by management.

Sanderson knew that awakening Porter and others to this perspective was crucial in his quest to develop leaders in the plant. It isn't only a matter of getting better results, but of putting people in positions to succeed and improve their own work based on well-designed, standardized processes.

Ironically, prior to Porter sharing the latest addition to his A3, Sanderson had pulled out a piece of crumpled paper with this quote: "We want to not only show respect to our people, the same way we want to show respect to everyone we meet in life, we also want to respect their humanity, what it is that makes us human, which is our ability to think and feel—we have to respect that humanity in the way we design the work, so that the work enables their very human characteristics to flourish."[4]

4. Speech by Fujio Cho, Toyota Chairman, 1997; John Shook translation.

Porter's Problem Analysis Tree—Lost in Translation

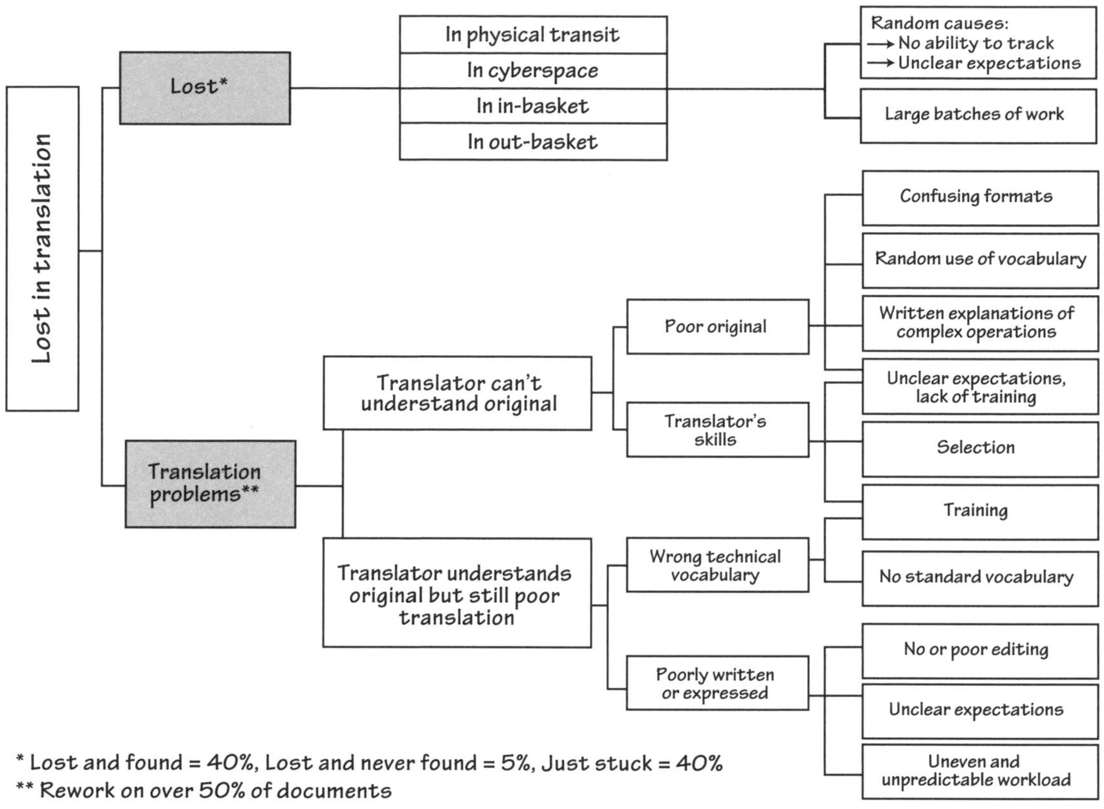

We want to not only show respect to our people, the same way we want to show respect to everyone we meet in life, we also want to respect their humanity, what it is that makes us human, which is our ability to think and feel—we have to respect that humanity in the way we design the work, so that the work enables their very human characteristics to flourish.[5]

—Fujio Cho

5. Speech by Fujio Cho, Toyota Chairman, 1997; John Shook translation.

Overall Process Analysis Tree

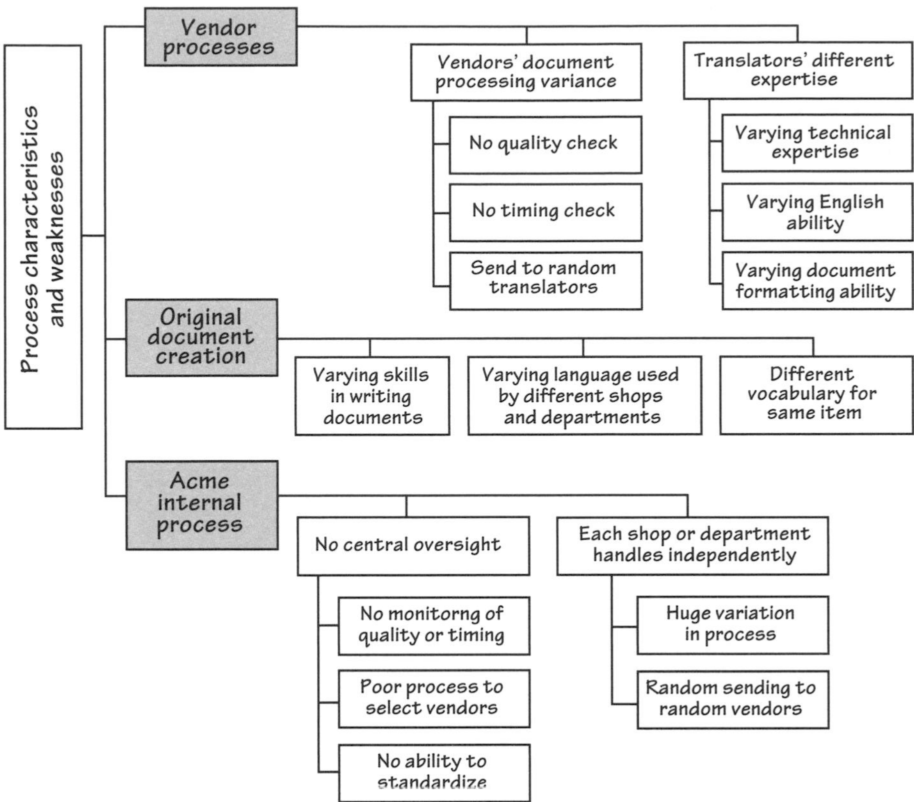

document creator that delayed the final delivery of the translated document (and therefore also drove up costs).

Everything pointed to improving quality and eliminating errors. Porter and his team created a current-state map, visualizing the process. This simple tool opened everyone's eyes to the problems (*see page 55*).[6] He stopped by Sanderson's desk and pointed to the latest revelation.

Cost overages come from rework, expediting, and overtime, most of which come from errors! Suddenly the problem was looking simple. He

The foundation for this mindset is developing a no-blame culture in which problems are brought into the light of day and not hidden for fear of retribution or embarrassment. This was key to the culture within Acme of people looking at problems *impersonally*. Importantly, however, a culture of "no blame" did not mean a culture of accepting problems that repeat without investigation nor one that would tolerate excuses: *no blame requires no excuses.*

6. For more on value-stream mapping, see: Mike Rother and John Shook, *Learning to See* (Cambridge, MA: Lean Enterprise Institute, 1999).

Porter's Current-State Map

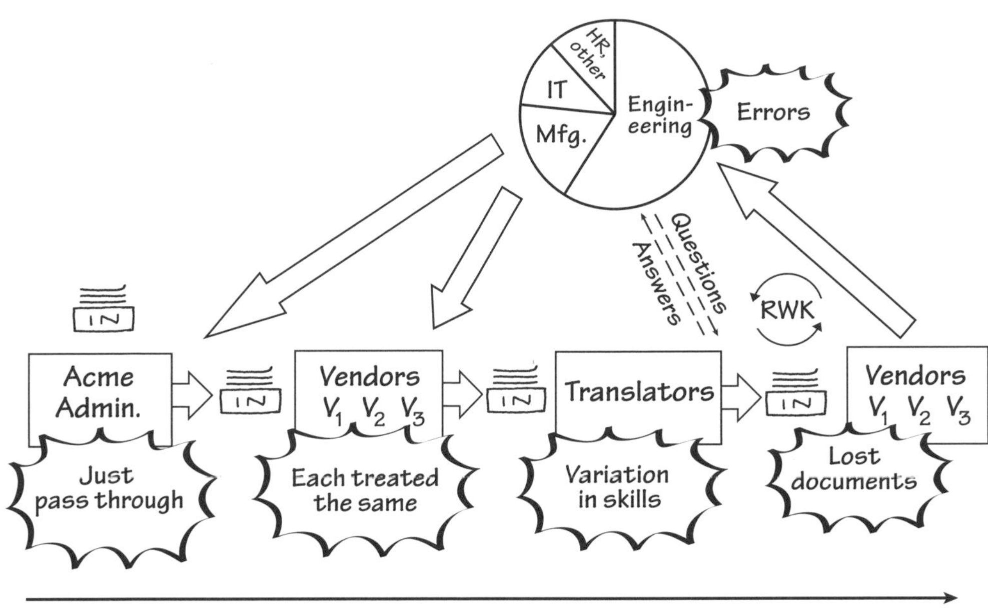

was excited as he shared his latest learning with Sanderson. "Good job," Sanderson acknowledged. "But why the huge difference in cost and lead time with the job-instruction documents?"

Porter was ready. The problem of documents getting lost was common to all types, but rework applied to job instructions at twice the rate of other types of documents. "It's an amplification of the problem that exists with the other materials —lack of clarity with the originals. The original documents are descriptions of the way work is performed; it is very hard to describe or translate precisely without seeing the actual work itself. Much of the content refers to subtle motions, tricks, or knacks in the way of doing the work."

In the case of document translation —as is usually the case—the problem wasn't the people but the system they worked in. Not only did Porter need to fix individual "single point" problems, he needed to fix the entire system. The way everything worked, the flow of work from beginning to end, the variation in the operation of each process, the fluctuation of workload and overburden placed on each individual worker, all contributed to the massive waste in the system.

Sanderson prodded Porter to continue: "What about the fact that all types of documents—not just job instructions—get lost?"

Again, Porter was ready. "The flow of documents is completely out of control. The documents move in big batches, and we know that batches always increase lead time and cause other problems, including workload fluctuations and items simply getting lost."

Sanderson nodded: "Great work. You've called out the problems, isolated the root causes, and begun to explore possible countermeasures. As you continue to analyze countermeasures that can be sustained," he added, "never forget to examine how the design of the work or the process created the variance or reason for the gap. The problem was produced by the work and can therefore be designed out."

"But that makes it sound as if whoever *designed* the work is responsible for all the problems and not the people who *do* the work. How does that fit with all the emphasis placed on individuals taking responsibility and initiative," Porter replied.

"In fact, it fits very well," Sanderson explained. "It's a matter of recognizing who's responsible for what or who can 'control' what. Look at it this way: As you know, a key operating principle of our company is simply to create value while eliminating waste."

"Waste or *muda*[7] is any action that adds time, effort, cost, but no value. Muda represents a problem for the organization and is usually caused or allowed by the design of the work

7. For more information on muda, see the *Lean Lexicon, Version 4.0*, edited by Chet Marchwinski, John Shook, and Alexis Schroeder (Cambridge, MA: Lean Enterprise Institute, 2008).

itself. Any work design that exhibits more than the minimum fluctuation or that overburdens people or processes will always lead to waste, such as delivery problems and errors. But the work can be redesigned so that errors and other problems can't easily occur. With the translation errors, individuals not taking appropriate responsibility may, in fact, be a contributing factor—but we won't know that until we complete the investigation. Only after you determine the root cause for the problems at hand will you be able to develop countermeasures that eliminate the root cause of your problem and close the gap."

Porter had seen it often in operations. It wasn't the operators, but the system that was causing problems. The document-translation process was no different.

Sanderson added, "You correctly point out that the responsibility to perform the work properly every time belongs with the person doing the work. Our responsibility is to design the work without overburden and fluctuation and to provide tools and training so that the person can successfully do their jobs, eliminate muda, and solve problems every time he or she does the job."

Finally, as Porter walked back to his desk, he had a true sense of confidence that he had accurately defined the situation, the goal, and the gap (the problem). The new title of the A3 reflected this reality—*Support launch objectives with accurate, timely document translation*—and focused not on creating a perfect translation process for its own sake, but on supporting its critical objectives. He set the A3 on his desk (*see pages 58–59*).

Porter had worked through his *Analysis* in detail, captured in an "interim A3"(*see pages 124–125*).

Key Questions

- Have you identified the real problem?
- Can you show the gap between the target and the current condition?
- Did you go to the gemba, observe, and talk to the people who do the work to fully grasp the current situation?
- Did you clarify the true business objectives?
- Did you uncover the right (i.e., most meaningful) information to support the analysis?
- Did you isolate the root cause(s) of the main components of the gap?
- Did you capture this material in the most clear and concise manner, i.e., one that clarifies true problems, invites analytic questions, and suggests direct countermeasures?

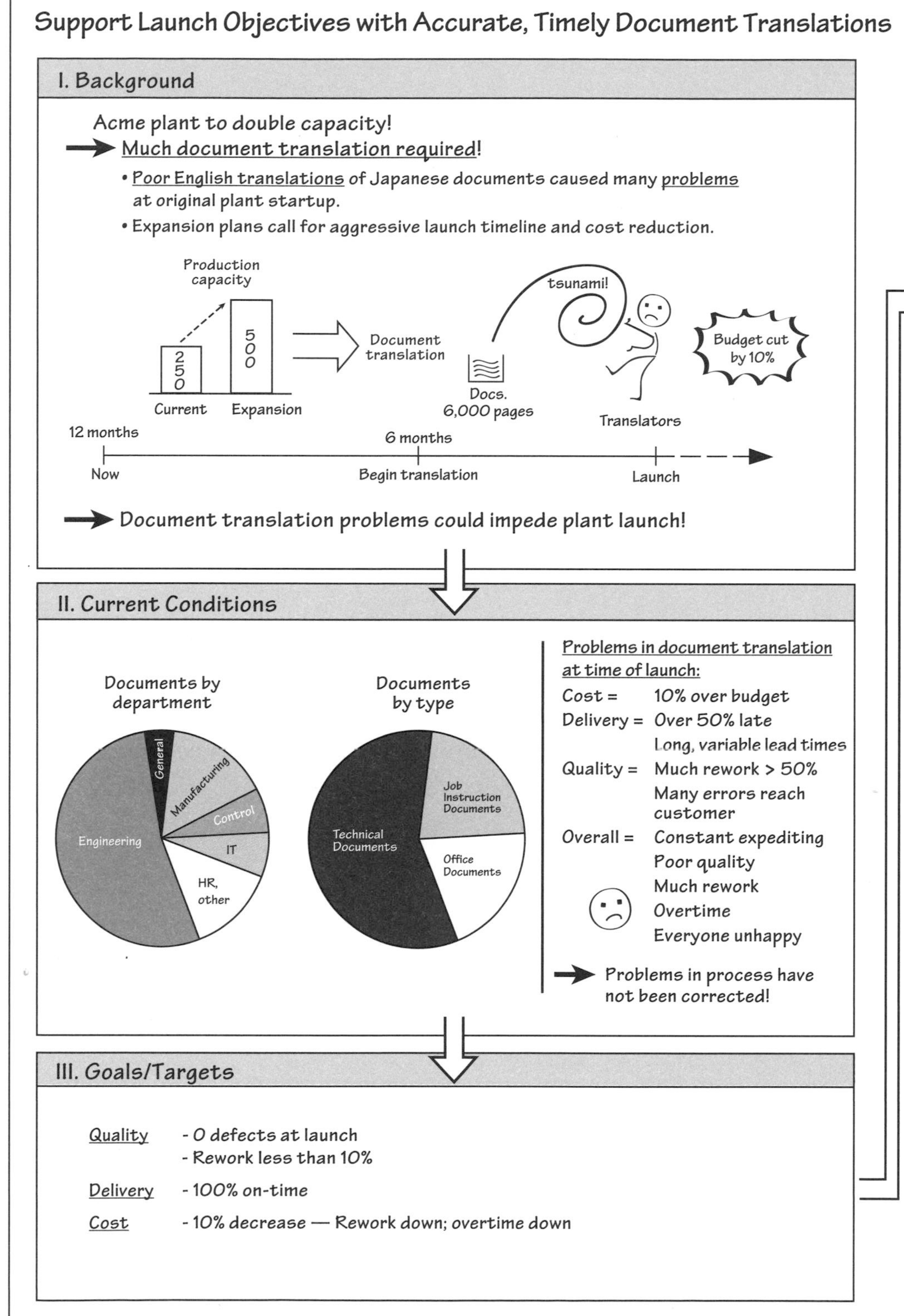
Support Launch Objectives with Accurate, Timely Document Translations
I. Background
Acme plant to double capacity!
Much document translation required!
• Poor English translations of Japanese documents caused many problems at original plant startup.
• Expansion plans call for aggressive launch timeline and cost reduction.
Production capacity
250
500
Current
Expansion
Document translation
tsunami!
Docs. 6,000 pages
Translators
Budget cut by 10%
12 months
Now
6 months
Begin translation
Launch
Document translation problems could impede plant launch!
II. Current Conditions
Documents by department
General
Manufacturing
Control
IT
HR, other
Engineering
Documents by type
Job Instruction Documents
Office Documents
Technical Documents
Problems in document translation at time of launch:
Cost = 10% over budget
Delivery = Over 50% late
Long, variable lead times
Quality = Much rework > 50%
Many errors reach customer
Overall = Constant expediting
Poor quality
Much rework
Overtime
Everyone unhappy
Problems in process have not been corrected!
III. Goals/Targets
Quality - 0 defects at launch
- Rework less than 10%
Delivery - 100% on-time
Cost - 10% decrease — Rework down; overtime down

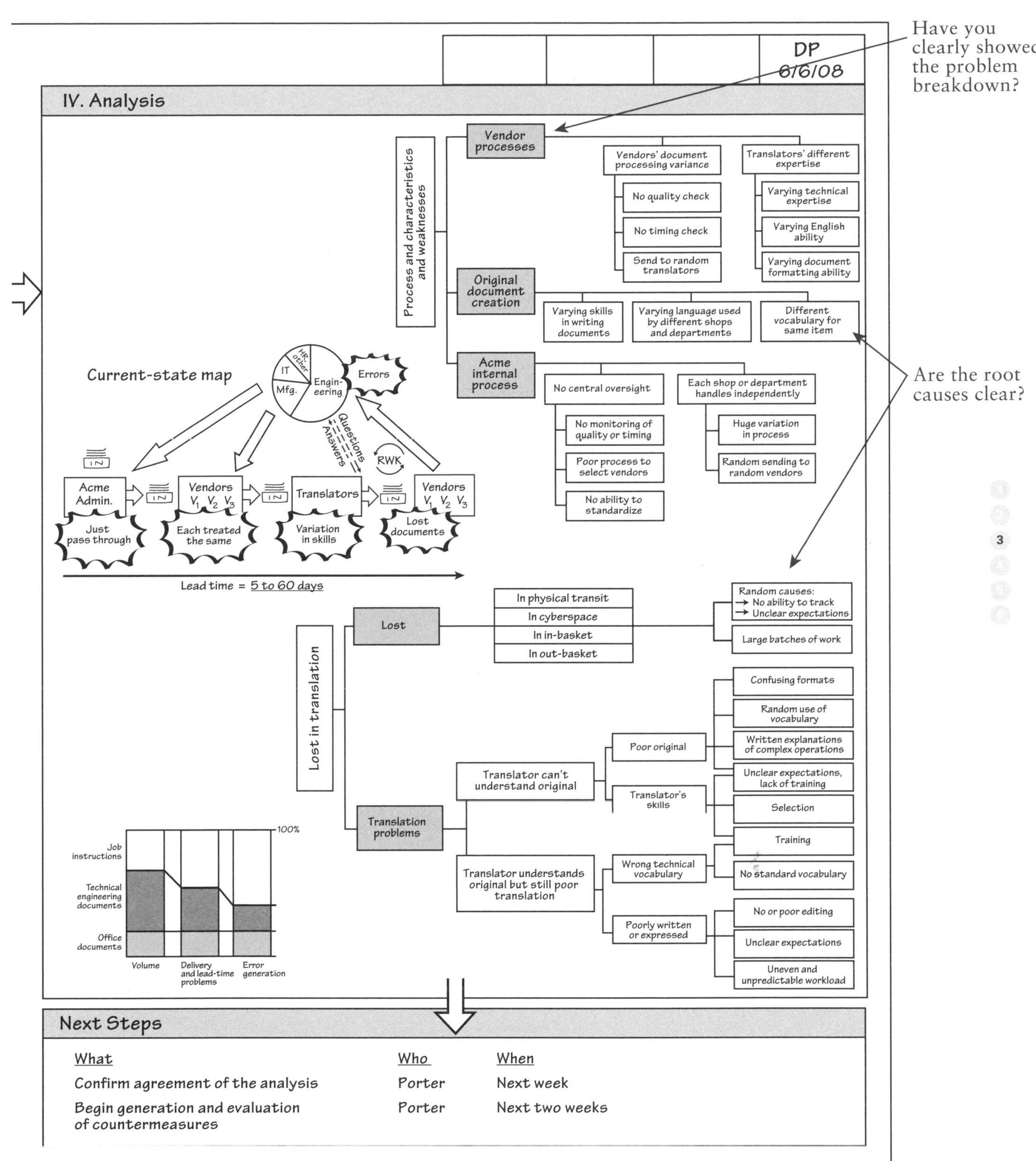
DP
6/6/08
IV. Analysis
Process and characteristics and weaknesses
Vendor processes
Vendors' document processing variance
No quality check
No timing check
Send to random translators
Translators' different expertise
Varying technical expertise
Varying English ability
Varying document formatting ability
Original document creation
Varying skills in writing documents
Varying language used by different shops and departments
Different vocabulary for same item
Acme internal process
No central oversight
No monitoring of quality or timing
Poor process to select vendors
No ability to standardize
Each shop or department handles independently
Huge variation in process
Random sending to random vendors
Current-state map
HR other
IT
Mfg.
Engineering
Errors
Questions
Answers
RWK
IN
Acme Admin.
Vendors V1 V2 V3
Translators
Just pass through
Each treated the same
Variation in skills
Lost documents
Lead time = 5 to 60 days
Lost in translation
Lost
In physical transit
In cyberspace
In in-basket
In out-basket
Random causes:
→ No ability to track
→ Unclear expectations
Large batches of work
Translation problems
Translator can't understand original
Poor original
Translator's skills
Translator understands original but still poor translation
Wrong technical vocabulary
Poorly written or expressed
Confusing formats
Random use of vocabulary
Written explanations of complex operations
Unclear expectations, lack of training
Selection
Training
No standard vocabulary
No or poor editing
Unclear expectations
Uneven and unpredictable workload
100%
Job instructions
Technical engineering documents
Office documents
Volume
Delivery and lead-time problems
Error generation
Next Steps
What
Who
When
Confirm agreement of the analysis
Porter
Next week
Begin generation and evaluation of countermeasures
Porter
Next two weeks
Have you clearly showed the problem breakdown?
Are the root causes clear?
3

Chapter 4
Proposed Countermeasures—Set-Based Decision-Making

Porter continues to learn how to develop, evaluate, and eventually select viable countermeasures that address the gap between the current and target conditions. He does this by going to the gemba, sharing his A3, and incorporating the feedback of individuals involved with the work. This enables him to propose specific actions designed to achieve outcomes and changes that will bring conditions closer to the target.

Sanderson continues to mentor Porter by constantly challenging and encouraging him to develop and test alternatives. Sanderson reminds himself of his important goal to inculcate A3 thinking that assesses goals and plans based on clear evaluation criteria.

As the process evolves from the initial learning phase to more tactical activity, Sanderson shifts his coaching of Porter to higher-level organizational and managerial concerns. Sanderson hopes to show Porter how the dialogue produced by the creation of alternative countermeasures can lead to organizational alignment and agreement, and how this is a necessary condition to transfer the basis for decision-making from *position-based authority* to *responsibility*. Concurrently, he has to show Porter that he doesn't need to be afraid of making mistakes and learning from them while at the same time exhibiting strong determination to lead the organization to success.

Porter's Progress

Now that Porter believed he had a firm grasp on the problems and root causes of the translation process, he was eager to turn his attention back to doing something about these issues. What countermeasure should he recommend?

Porter sorted through the different ideas he had uncovered so far. The experience had taught him that few problems are easily "fixed," since repairing any defect without correcting the root cause can simply push the problem elsewhere. This had occurred in the past when translators occasionally took it upon themselves to "correct" an original Japanese document, only to remove a nuance that was then never translated, resulting in serious mistakes in the actual production work performed in the plant.[1]

Porter had learned that while specific problems may appear to be distinct and with easily isolated or special causes, they often serve as a lens, which collects and expands a wide range of actions and processes. This was proving to be the case with the translation process. The more Porter spoke with each of the individuals involved in the work, the more he saw underlying and interconnected problems, and the more ways he found to improve parts of the system that then might impact the other parts.

After considering all the ideas and recommendations he had gathered, Porter continued to work on his A3. In the *Proposed Countermeasures* section he wrote a series of action items to standardize the vocabulary used by Acme for all of its technical documents. He felt strongly that this approach would produce the greatest

Mentoring Mind

Sanderson was conflicted.

He had resisted the natural impulse to step in with specific recommendations to Porter as he developed countermeasures through his conversations with workers involved in the process. Sanderson had also fought back the urge to intervene between Porter and employees, who occasionally complained directly to Sanderson when they tired of seeing Porter, A3 in hand, coming their way again.

Sanderson could see the direction that Porter's proposal was heading and it made him uneasy. Porter was showing progress, and his current A3 was a solid approach—to parts of the overall translation problem. This was a mix of good and bad.

Porter's current A3 showed much better thinking about the problems, in both depth (getting to the root causes) and breadth (looking across the organization). But Porter was still confused about how to tie his proposal to the actual problem causes.

Sanderson and Porter had arrived at a hazardous point in their learning journey. They had made progress, but had a huge distance yet to travel. Sanderson sought to keep Porter motivated, while forcing him to review and revise his work.

1. For more on this see: Peter M. Senge, Art Kleiner, Charlotte Roberts, Rick Ross, Bryan Smith, "Fixes that Backfire," *The Fifth Discipline Fieldbook: Strategies and Tools for Building a Learning Organization*, (New York: Doubleday, 1994).

overall improvements. This companywide common vocabulary would eliminate the confusion created by the ambiguity of different job sites referring to identical processes with different language. For example, a press is a stamping machine—except when it's a verb meaning to apply pressure to attach one component to another. That one was relatively easy, but others could be highly specific and situational: one textile loom's *bobbin* is another's *pirn*.

A common vocabulary would eliminate confusion at the source. It could stir up productive dialogue among workers about the details of their work. It would certainly facilitate smoother translations.

Under the general heading of "Produce Glossary of Standard Vocabulary" he wrote down three steps for getting it done:

1. Gather all the specifications and definitions used in every Acme job site.
2. Review them as a whole to see which terms could be improved and ultimately standardized.
3. Roll out the new vocabulary gradually under Porter's supervision.

Porter thought this was a realistic solution that took into account the nature of the work and the feedback of the workers. He was hopeful that Sanderson would approve.

Sanderson realized that Porter was discouraged to find that his breakthroughs seemed to do no more than make new problems visible. So he continued to focus Porter on the A3 way of learning, and compliment him when his approach to an issue was well-structured. But he didn't offer forced praise on problem specifics, much less on solutions. This would be as harmful as unjustly criticizing him.

Managing by A3 often stretched Sanderson's patience, but also provided a structure to stay on course—patiently—when he felt the urge to rush ahead. He had to control the urge to praise individual "fixes." The desire to celebrate heroic campaigns remained a perennial threat to the necessary daily mindset of looking for small problems and anomalies as opportunities for constant improvement. Moreover, Sanderson naturally wanted at times to simply tell Porter what to do—yet recognized that in so doing he would be acting in a manner that contradicted his message of assuming responsibility.

Such insights could only be learned, as opposed to taught. At no other time was his coaching approach to Porter more critical.

Not So Fast

Sanderson's brow furrowed as he spoke, "Your proposal addresses important aspects of the problem—and I am confident that it would, in fact, improve the current state. There is a lot of good information here. However …"

Porter had become familiar with Sanderson's "however," and braced himself for what he knew was coming.

"However," continued Sanderson, "this still doesn't address the problem thoroughly. What you've done here is come up with what is probably a good approach to a large and important problem. But I'm confused about the link between all that you've unearthed and your suggestion for making the translation process work better. You haven't provided a basis for a compelling plan for action."

"But I have!" Porter replied, with frustration. He was irritated at being constantly told to go back, try again, withhold judgment, and not jump to conclusions. He had found a solution that he felt should work, and had gone through numerous iterations to make it doable. Now he felt eager to get it done, and wanted to be through with this game of grasshopper and sensei. "Listen. Why can't we just roll out this plan and improve it as we go? It feels ready to me."

"Not so fast," said Sanderson, trying to defuse Porter's attachment to this one approach and keep him engaged in discovery. "What we have here is a pretty good proposal with a good approach to the cause of some of the problems. You have identified a good technical approach to the root cause of some of the problems. But how much of the gap between the current and target

Options to Explore before Solutions to Defend

Sanderson encouraged all A3 authors to prepare a set of countermeasures for others to assess, regardless of how certain they are that one specific plan represents the best solution. Presenting numerous options improves the quality of the dialogue and spurs further learning.

Porter was beginning to realize that his job was to explore opportunities and ideas from which a good decision could be made. He needed to produce viable options, and not simply as a means of creating the best countermeasures. Showing options would help build buy-in from everybody. Involving all the right people and cross-functional groups in the process would lay the groundwork for implementation, since the plan itself would incorporate the input of people doing the work. *Going to the gemba can produce shared ownership as well as knowledge.*

Sanderson was getting Porter to see on his own that assessing the relative value of different options rather than judging just one proposal—his own—helps A3 owners to behave more impartially and with greater objectivity.

Lobbying for one solution invariably involves a selective use of data. Presenting a set of options enables Porter and others to shift their focus from seeking closure to exploring the state will be removed through developing the standard vocabulary? How much lead-time reduction do you anticipate? How many errors will it prevent?"

Sanderson paused, and the two of them studied the A3 in silence until he continued. "Let's work backward—show me what your gemba investigation has revealed to be the real cause of the problem. Then we can assess the viability of this as a countermeasure."

"How do you know that this *isn't* the best countermeasure?" Porter asked, becoming exasperated.

relative merits of as many reasonable alternatives as possible. And equally important, especially to the changing role of Porter, the deeper explanation of choices helps others understand the facts the A3 owner has uncovered. It gives Porter credibility.

Once Porter investigates deeply enough to propose a set of countermeasures, he will become Acme's authority on the problem at hand—document translation. And Porter's

4

Countermeasures vs. Solutions

A3 proposals typically use the term "countermeasure" rather than "solution." Like homicide detectives who refer to cases as "closed" (meaning that a suspect has been identified based on evidence and handed over to the courts) rather than "solved" (a condition that is rarely fully satisfied in the real world), A3 owners seek countermeasures to problems instead of permanent solutions.

The term "countermeasure" refers to the way proposed actions are directly addressed to existing conditions. More important, the wording recognizes that even apparent "solutions" inevitably create new problems. They are merely "temporary responses to specific problems that will serve until a better approach is found or conditions change."[2] Every plan, and in fact every tool, set of tools, or operating practice, can be seen as a countermeasure that is subject to change or even elimination as conditions change and evolve in the workplace. Once a countermeasure is in place, it will create a new situation, with its own set of problems that will require their own countermeasures.

2. Steven J. Spear, "Learning to Lead at Toyota," *Harvard Business Review*, September–October 1999.

"I don't," Sanderson replied, trying to be patient. "And that's a good question because from what I see, you don't know this either. Let's try again. How much of the problem will go away if you implement your proposal?

"Well, I can't really say."

"You've uncovered a great many useful facts," said Sanderson. "You identified several root causes, correct? Work from those root causes out—they will lead you to effective countermeasures. Never try to retrofit a solution because it looks good.

"You've generated some good ideas. But is this all you've come up with? What about the other problems that aren't addressed by your countermeasures? Don't others involved in the process have ideas? Equally important, how have the others reacted to your ideas?"

"I can see," Sanderson continued, "that you have learned to develop the technical knowledge needed to address the problem, without which we wouldn't even be having this conversation. But as you think ahead to the tactical process of implementing change, it's time to explore the different approaches in greater detail.

"In fact," added Sanderson, "rather than continue to discuss the merits of any one countermeasure or recommendation, let's shift the way we go about thinking about what we should do next. Please revise your A3. And when you bring it back, be sure to provide a *set* of countermeasures—a variety of approaches to the problem—with at least one countermeasure tied to each major root cause. From that set we can discuss the best approach. There is no need to lock in on one solution yet."

A3 should reflect the facts he has discovered rather than the solution he concluded was ideal. Sharing different fact-based approaches to the problem enables Sanderson—and for that matter any other reader of the A3 —to learn what Porter has learned.

From reading as well as writing many A3s, Sanderson knew this was a pure way to generate fact-based dialogue based on the fullest grasp of the current state. All parties assess the situation with the necessary detachment needed to make a good decision. From such a perspective, Porter's emerging organizational battles would subside.

Gathering Ideas

Porter saw that he needed to incorporate the thinking of others who had valid concerns about the problem and to include alternatives that would address the issues they raised. And so, Porter again found himself rewriting his A3. He put all the ideas he had gathered so far into a table and headed back to the gemba, taking his draft A3, soliciting feedback, and testing ideas. A number of ideas emerged from dialogues at the gemba:

- Frances, the procurement specialist in Purchasing, was still eager to source the document-translation work through a competitive bid process, selecting the lowest-cost vendor.
- Translators suggested creating a standard set of definitions for every activity and tool that might require translation. This was the countermeasure Porter singled out in his previous draft, which had been challenged by Sanderson. Porter still felt that this countermeasure could have the biggest impact.
- Engineers in the Acme shops had recommended to Porter that they retrain all translators to ensure that each person handling the work would be adept at understanding the technical details of the document and the nuances of local idiom. Porter saw this suggestion as an attempt to standardize the work of translators.
- Porter had given a lot of thought to the issues of documents getting lost or stuck and the unpredictable lead times. He observed that handoffs could be handled more seamlessly and the overall flow of documents facilitated more effectively by creating a central document-flow and tracking process with the status of all documents visible for everyone to see.

Organizational Currency

As Sanderson considered Porter's changing role as the A3 progressed, he thought about how to help him navigate this new terrain.

Shifting from investigating the problem (the left side of the A3) to exploring the best countermeasures was a different kind of problem for Porter, one that required a new level of coaching. Until now, Sanderson had focused on developing Porter as a problem-solver. The coaching and questioning centered on learning how to see problems and how to distinguish problems and root causes from solutions.

Now that Porter had worked through the problem to determine root causes and was beginning to think about countermeasures, he was also encountering the first wave of organizational resistance. This was just another problem—one of a different type to be sure—that required the same type of problem-solving approach and skills that Porter had learned to apply to the specific business problem of the document-translation process.

Sanderson realized it was time to shift the focus of his coaching to these organizational or people issues, which can often seem so messy and insurmountable. Now he needed to coach Porter through the upcoming process of using the A3 to gain agreement, to achieve organizational alignment.

- One of the vendors used a three-step process in which each document would go through a sequence of 1) basic translation, 2) bilingual check, and 3) thorough editing and rewrite by a native English-speaking technical writer. This process could be used by all vendors.
- Similarly, another vendor would sometimes segment the distribution or flow of documents according to the type of document, as divided into three categories: 1) policy or office documents (written in prose), 2) technical engineering documents, and 3) descriptive documents that explained the way work is done, such as standardized work charts and job instructions.
- The Production Department suggested insourcing all or most of the translation work. Internal translators would be able to learn the actual work and should therefore be able to create better, more accurate work descriptions. (The cost could also be expected to be lower. However, Acme was very cautious about adding full-time employees for work that was shorter-term, project-based.)
- As an alternative countermeasure to the troublesome job-instruction documents, Carter, lead technical documentation engineer, suggested integrating digital photos and even video into the original documents, which would help the translators understand the nuances of the descriptions of the work and provide better English explanations.
- Rick and Terry suggested the purchase of an automated translation software package. This idea surprised Porter. If workable, it could constitute the most dramatic improvement of all. (A quick trial later, however, proved it to be impractical for Acme's translation requirements.)

Porter had difficulty in such situations in the past, and would need to learn how to manage such cross-organizational, people issues.

But Sanderson could only be so patient with his approach, since the Acme plant expansion was beginning to run out of time—a fact that was becoming an intense topic of conversation between Sanderson and his own boss.

Sanderson was tempted to protect Porter from some of the political confrontations that his A3 research provoked, but Porter and others needed to learn these lessons on their own. Most importantly, he hoped that Porter would continue to improve his thinking based on the direct feedback he received from the process of testing out potential countermeasures. Bringing conflict down to these practical levels could minimize the confrontations that often dominated planning, problems, and decisions.

Porter had focused on just one solution, just as he had done prior to his process of thorough root-cause analysis. This was a problem and lightning rod for political rebuke.

The quality of this proposal wasn't the issue: There was no evidence that Porter had considered alternatives and the opinions and ideas of others. Either they had not been involved in this process or their suggestions somehow did not make their way into

Nemawashi

Porter's practice of gaining consensus for his countermeasures taps into *nemawashi*. This Japanese term consists of two ideas, "ne" or root with "mawashi" or twist, and refers to the idea that before you can put a plant in entirely new soil, you must pull it up with its roots intact so it can take root in its new location and ensure organic and sustained growth. Literally translated as "preparing the ground for planting."

On a broad level, nemawashi refers to the consensus-building process of aligning the organization around broad or specific goals. The A3 process supports, and indeed recapitulates, this practice on a smaller fractal level. As managers share and improve A3s through dialogue with individuals, they seed the garden for progress and improvement. Garnering the ideas and input of the participants helps ensure that the final decision has grown naturally from the work as naturally as a plant from well-tilled soil. Approval at the end of the process becomes, essentially, a formality (resulting, for example, in short meetings in which much of the work has been done, rather than contentious and agenda-fueled gatherings where decisions are subject to many variables).

This same dynamic applies to hoshin kanri (variously translated as "strategy/policy deployment" or "strategy alignment/management"),[3] which refers to the process of creating alignment around objectives and actions from the top of the company down to the work-group level, while at the same time bubbling ideas and initiatives from the bottom up or middle out. Aggressive goals at the executive level are realized as measurable objectives throughout the organization, just as Porter's work on translation supports Sanderson's goals for the plant expansion startup. Senior management objectives become more specific and measurable as they cascade to the front lines, while progress reports and new ideas flow upward from the lower levels to the senior executives.

3. For more information see: Pascal Dennis, *Getting the Right Things Done* (Cambridge, MA: Lean Enterprise Institute, 2006).

Porter had methodically taken his A3 to the gemba again and shared what he had learned. He reached for his pencil every time someone came up with a new idea, which he would capture immediately on the A3. The more he tracked down the source of delays, sloppiness, and overwork, the more his report generated solid recommendations.

As a result, his new A3 now contained a choice of countermeasures. Porter continued to believe that standardizing the vocabulary would yield the greatest long-term benefits. Yet he proposed a set of countermeasures, each of them detailed, practical, and targeted directly at the root causes of existing problems. His A3 got stronger as he continued to shop it around the company.

Porter talked with engineers who wrote specifications. He spoke with Frances and others in Purchasing who were charged with reducing costs for all indirect services, such as translation, janitorial services, and payroll. He spoke again with the individuals in IT who had helped create online forms and managed the systems that handled the heavy traffic of engineering and other documents. He talked to shopfloor leaders and workers who used the final documents.

But the more that Porter explored ideas that got into the finer details of how people got their work done, the greater the degree of turf wars and general organizational push-back or resistance he encountered: individuals in different shops who still resented his meddling, and managers of these shops who proved passively unhelpful.

this A3. More groundwork was required—more conversations, more information, more feedback, more involvement from everyone that would be asked to help solve the problem or work the project.

Sanderson believed that Porter's proposal could produce significant benefit, but it needed to reflect the input of the people actually doing the work. He needed Porter to see the A3 as a form of *organizational currency* —an accepted and commonly understood form of sharing and discussing important information. The A3 report must be a live document designed to trigger productive dialogue. The more it's based on facts and ideas from those affected and linked to clear countermeasures, the less likely anyone would try to undermine the process.

But this also began to provoke yet another critical point in Sanderson's journey as mentor to Porter. Some of the ideas being generated were solutions serving the personal convenience of the proposer. There is a clear line between *engaging* the organization and merely acquiescing to the demands of everyone. Sanderson was determined to facilitate Porter's mastery of learning the balance between addressing everyone's concerns and exercising good judgment and leadership.

The degree of negative reaction puzzled him more than frustrated him. After all, Acme was a pretty good, lean company and a model for many best practices in its industry. People should be, well, *above* this sort of thing—shouldn't they?

Often he felt that his work, produced with the best intentions, was merely making him enemies. He wasn't trying to meddle or boss people around, he was simply trying to learn more about the nitty-gritty details of the process and come up with a solution that would help everyone.

Just as Sanderson knew enough about the document-translation process to ask questions regarding Porter's search for problems, he also had gathered enough information and had spoken with enough plant personnel to see the buzzsaws into which Porter was headed. Could Porter gather ideas without losing his head—or ideas that he firmly believed in?

Sanderson encouraged Porter to never discard information, regardless of how much he might disagree with it. On the contrary, embrace all reasonable ideas, but then let the ideas, the facts, speak for themselves.

One contentious topic was the idea of standardizing vocabulary. It sounded great on the surface, the translators loved it, and it seemed to make sense to most people. But the Acme engineers and others who generated the original documents were up in arms.

"Why should we change our work just to accommodate the translators," the engineers argued. "They're supposed to be working for us, not the other way around." It was relatively easy for Porter to address that concern by explaining that the standard vocabulary would benefit everyone involved, not just the translators.

A second concern of the engineers was tougher to deal with. Since different document creators used different vocabulary, who should decide what the final "official" terminology should be? "I've used this term for 20 years," said one Acme veteran. "Why should I be the one to change?" Engineers in many departments argued the same point.

Porter could put this concept into practice by running trials of the various ideas he had gathered from the gemba. If the ideas performed badly or completely failed the trial, he won't be insulting those that generated an idea by rejecting it. They along with Porter would see the trial result for themselves.

In doing so, Porter would eventually reach the right set of countermeasures and have the backing of those who generated ideas—even those whose ideas were no longer being considered.

And so while Porter's A3 with one solution was entirely inappropriate, so was Porter's desire to address everyone else's concerns while abandoning his own.

Porter Gives In

Eager to get on with things and mindful of Sanderson's direction to be inclusive of the ideas and views of the people who work in the process, Porter revised his A3 accordingly, dropping the standard vocabulary as a countermeasure, even though he believed it was the best idea. He decided that trying to formally push such an ambitious change as standardizing vocabulary would create substantial resistance.

He created a set of six countermeasures:

1. *Central document-flow tracking process*: Develop means of monitoring and managing the flow and timing of documents.
2. *Three-step process*: Develop and implement standard flow process at vendors.
3. *Competitive bid process*: Create a bid package, distribute to vendors, and select the best bid(s).
4. *Automate*: Purchase software; assign editor.
5. *In-source:* Hire professional translator as full-time employee.
6. *Standard format with digital visuals*: Incorporate images, which should be especially beneficial for troublesome job-instruction documents.

Porter met with Sanderson, who was surprised to see the changes: "What happened to the standard vocabulary countermeasure?"

"Well, some people didn't like the idea."

"So, you just dropped it?" asked Sanderson.

"Yes. It didn't seem worth it."

"So, why are some people opposing it?"

Productive Conflict

Porter's decision to drop a potentially powerful countermeasure out of a desire to avoid conflict was a completely understandable reaction. Earlier in his career, when Sanderson first took on more of a leadership role at Acme, he had found himself making decisions on the basis of what he thought others wanted, rather than on what was clearly the best response to the matter at hand. Few of these choices led to positive change.

Finally one of his mentors took him aside to help clarify his thinking. "You must call waste 'waste,'" explained his sensei. While there were situations in which polite etiquette was useful (such as getting to know one another or dealing with cultural differences), making good decisions required everyone's complete commitment to dealing with harsh reality.

This produced yet another counter-intuitive aspect of A3 management: respect *through* conflict. Asking someone "How do you know?" was not an effort to question the person's judgment, but an attempt to discuss, understand, and test their thinking.

In this context, respect did not mean shying away from conflicting opinions or bruised feelings. Respect meant treating individuals as competent workers who, with the right tools and the right system, could display

"Well," Porter explained, "they said they didn't like the idea of changing the way they do things just to make work easier for a vendor."

"Really? Did you explain how it would help us and help them, as well?"

"Yes," Porter responded, "and that seemed to help. But they still didn't like the idea. No one wants to change the way they do things, like the terminology they use. They want others to change."

"That's a response to be expected," said Sanderson. "Did you explain how the process would work, how you would decide which terms to use? Do you *know* how you will decide?"

"No," Porter replied, feeling a little chagrined. "And that seemed like another reason to look elsewhere. It seems like a very difficult countermeasure to implement."

"So you gave up?" asked Sanderson, pointedly.

"Well, yes," said Porter, "it just seemed too hard, and, more importantly, it seemed to go against your advice to include the ideas of others."

"OK, it's good that you showed respect for the ideas of others. However, how can the organization decide the best course of action for the company when you've already decided to leave out important ideas because you felt they might be too difficult, or because someone didn't like the idea? When you discard an idea out of hand, you deprive others of the opportunity to explore and evaluate it."

their full capabilities. And if challenging them with facts, pushing them to explain their thinking, and refusing to accept suboptimal results made folks discouraged or angry, so be it.

Eventually they would see that this approach represented a more complete and enduring form of respect than any short-term concession. In a system designed to produce lasting countermeasures, solving problems with soothing words but no meaningful changes would prove no more lasting than any other quick fix.

Set-Based Decision-Making

One of the most important aspects of lean decision-making involves the assessment of a set of potential countermeasures rather than just one approach. By exploring a range of potential choices, individuals can uncover a broader and more meaningful database for analysis. They can minimize risk by running a wider range of potential scenarios. And through quick, simple trials, they save costs by preventing large projects from having to make large-scale change late in the process as a result of choosing a weak approach early on.

The practice of developing multiple choices can be seen clearly in Toyota's product development process, where a set-based approach to decision-making represents a fundamentally different approach from the common "point-based design" model of most manufacturers. Rather than lock into an early design choice and then go through countless prototypes and iterations from this one point, Toyota developers simultaneously consider numerous solutions before deciding on the best option. "Toyota explores the space of possible design before making important decisions," argues Al Ward, pointing out that premature closure risks missing critical facts.[3]

Delaying the decision on critical dimensions of a product until the right time enables a company to ensure that customers' expectations are fully understood, that they will be satisfied by the product design, and that the design is, in fact, manufactureable. In this type of system the manager's job is *to prevent people from making decisions too quickly.*

Such an approach applies equally to decisions on all projects. The responsibility of the individual developing the options is not to create the ideal "solution" that can be iterated to perfection, rather it is to help everyone involved in the work to develop the fullest understanding of the current situation and the most effective set of countermeasures. This puts the group in the position of making the best decision based on the fullest set of facts.

3. Allen Ward, Jeffrey K. Liker, John J. Cristiano, and Durward Sobek II, "The Second Toyota Paradox: How Delaying Decisions Can Make Better Cars Faster," *Sloan Management Review,* Spring 1995.

   Allen Ward, *Lean Product and Process Development* (Cambridge, MA: Lean Enterprise Institute, 2007).

Set-Based Decision-Making

Porter gazed upon his A3, examining the rigor and logic of its components, reviewing every last detail. And then aggressively erased the *Proposed Countermeasures* section once again.

Porter was dizzy from swinging from extreme to extreme. He had learned that championing *one* approach had prevented him from including more perspectives into his earlier plan, weakened his analysis of the root cause and potential countermeasures, and even created adversaries. He had been so determined to fix the problem and so eager to show everyone he was on top of matters, he had stubbornly settled on what he considered the *single* best approach and then organized every bit of information to serve this goal.

Then he had learned from Sanderson's counsel to change his approach. "Don't show me exactly how you intend to fix the problem, but continue to think like a scientist, pursuing multiple alternatives simultaneously," Sanderson said. "The most important issue now is not what you propose, but how you think through the true nature of the issues and implications of different ideas. To decide among those ideas, take a set-based approach to presenting them to the organization and evaluating them."

That's when Porter went overboard in the other direction and accepted carte blanche push-back from the organization that resulted in a proposal that eliminated an important countermeasure, the creation of a standard vocabulary. He could not adopt everyone's precise ideas and nuances, but he needed to address their concerns and present alternative paths for improvement. And addressing this did not necessarily mean trying to make everyone 100% happy.

Process Rules

Sanderson was happy with Porter's progress in some ways. One sign of his learner's development was that Sanderson found himself less involved with Porter on a day-to-day basis, as Porter focused his energy more on delving into the work and mastering the details, reporting back frequently, in short exchanges, effectively asking clear questions, and taking advice easily.

While Porter had not exactly created the perfect plan, he had learned how to use the process of planning to include everyone in what needed to happen. Sanderson knew that he would soon discover the additional challenges of testing this through experiments.

Sanderson wasn't entirely comfortable with some aspects of Porter's recommendations. He knew he wouldn't do it quite this way if he were the owner of the proposal. But it was Desi Porter and not Ken Sanderson who owned the problem, who was presenting a business case, and who was engaged in the hard work of doing everything necessary to gain agreement from everyone concerned.

This was a critical distinction, one that was recognized by the executive leadership and had become part of the corporate culture of Acme. "Consensus" or agreement did not mean that everyone had equal voice in every instance, or that every stake-

Walking the gemba had been a humbling yet exciting process of learning from the people doing the work. Porter realized that his criteria for picking the best approach should be guided by the new theme of the A3: *Support launch objectives with accurate, timely document translations.* This meant developing a process that would consistently eliminate the greatest amount of waste and problems, while boosting effectiveness and efficiency.

Porter regarded the input of everyone as a force of momentum, carrying the plan toward implementation. With the help of those touching the process, Porter had now created a target-state map, showing how Porter, Frances, Ana, engineers, and others wanted the process to work.

His A3 proposal was again revised to include a grouping of the root causes into just three buckets focused around the general causes of a) documents getting lost or stuck, b) document-translation problems due to poor originals, and c) document-translation problems due to issues in the work of the translators. Porter also included a complete list and evaluation of all the countermeasures, currently under consideration, including steps to begin a standardized vocabulary (*see Porter's Countermeasure Matrix on page 79*).

holder would do it the same way were he or she in charge. Consensus meant that there was an identified owner of the issue; that the owner had submitted a reasonable proposal following an accepted process that had engaged the knowledge, ideas, and interests of the stakeholders; and that these stakeholders agreed to support the owner in attaining the desired outcome.

Consensus/Agreement

Does:

- Recognize the owner
- Who has submitted a reasonable approach (A3) that:
  - Reflects the engaging thinking and reasonable concerns of all stakeholders
  - Who agree to support the owner to attainment.

Does not:

- Mean unanimity,
- Majority rule, or
- "I agree because that's how I would do it."

Porter's Problem Analysis Tree—Three Root-Cause Groupings

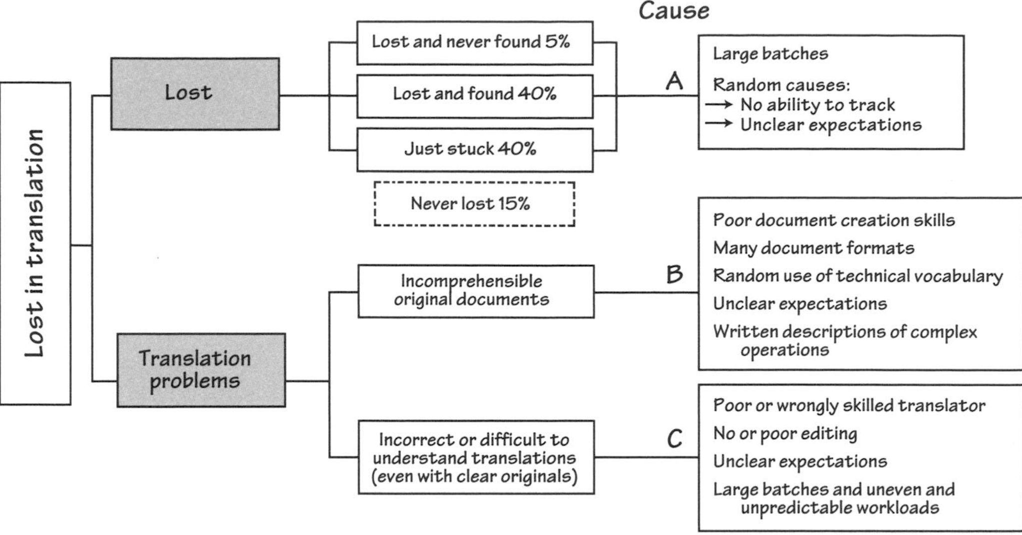

Porter worked through the list of many root causes, grouping them into three common issues: a) lost documents, b) translation problems due to problematic originals, and c) translation problems due to a poor translation process.

Porter's Target-state Map

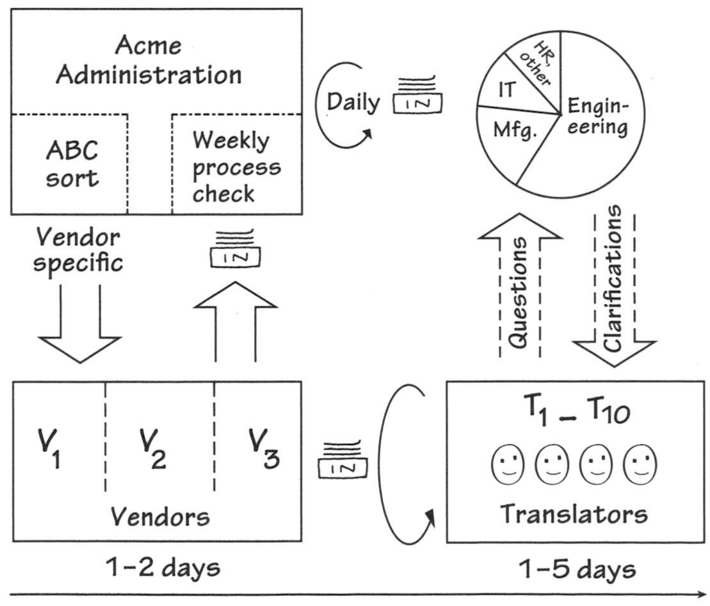

Porter's target-state map shows systemic countermeasures for the major problems present in the current state. Daily takeaway and delivery will ensure level workload and, along with the weekly process check, timely tracking of the movement of documents at each step through the system.

Porter's Countermeasure Matrix

Countermeasure	Description	Eval.	Benefit
Central document-flow tracking process	Overall process ownership established Document flow and timing management - Timing control chart; weekly check - Flow segmentation by document type: "A, B, C sort" - Level and steady flow of documents (no peak)	◉	Delivery, quality, cost
Standard vocabulary database	Standard terms for processes, equipment, tools, and work used across job sites Gathered from each department and input into database for use by internal document creators and translators	◉	Quality
Standard template with digital visuals	Create standard templates; include photos or videos to illustrate difficult-to-describe work	◉	Quality
Standard vendor three-step process	Step 1: Translation by topic specialist Step 2: Rewrite by native English speaker Step 3: Check by highly skilled bilingual	○	Quality, delivery
Competitive bid process	Develop, distribute bid package, select best bid(s). Concerns: Bid will show only lowest piece price (Led by Procurement)	△	Cost
Automation	Utilize translator software for some document types Concerns: Quality, rework (Led by IT department)	△	Cost (?)
Insource	Hire full-time, in-house translator for troublesome job-instruction documents Concerns: Cost, long-term HR obligations	X	Quality, delivery

◉ Outstanding ○ Good △ Questionable but possibly adequate X No good

Porter believed his list of proposed countermeasures now encompassed input from all involved in the process—including his own desire for a standard vocabulary—and addressed the three groupings of root causes. The team's review of options (the evaluation column) was beginning to show a clearer path of action.

From Investigator to Advocate

"Tell me more about your cost-saving recommendation," Sanderson requested of Porter as he studied the latest revision of the A3. "What would change if we implemented these methods?"

"I believe that in the first year we would reduce costs by at least 10% as a result of eliminating expedited shipping costs and avoiding delays," Porter replied. "We would easily recoup any investment in new training or systems."

"Yes, I can see the benefits in terms of costs," Sanderson said, continuing to review the A3.

"I can give you a breakdown of this. We've done a spreadsheet," said Porter as he rifled through his papers.

"Yes, that's excellent work," Sanderson replied. "But let's take a step back once more. Your insights into the process have revealed where we can save money. But does this plan directly attack the source of the recurring waste? Would it eliminate what is causing the delays, errors, and rework?"

"I think the only way to truly fix the process is to fix the root cause of all the quality problems, the reasons for the generation of the errors," said Porter. "If the errors can be eliminated, the rework eliminated, then the biggest impediment to meeting the delivery requirements will be eliminated. It will be a lot of work up front, on the part of many people, but our trials have shown that the improvement in first-run quality will pay off in the long run."

With that Sanderson stood up. He even slapped Porter on the shoulder.

Shifting Gears

If you become a teacher, by your pupils you'll be taught.[4] While this snippet from one of his favorite musicals was a bit corny, thought Sanderson, it could not have been more fitting. As he examined the most recent set of recommendations from Porter, Sanderson realized that his charge had indeed thrown himself so fully into the process that his technical knowledge of the situation far exceeded his own.

Sure, there was still work to do. He could see a number of unintended consequences that could result from any one of these actions. Yet these concerns came from his own experience, not directly from the current information reflected in this plan.

It was time, Sanderson realized, to change the focus of Porter's efforts in this project, as well as his own. He needed to shift from challenging technical and logistical details to assessing the ability of Porter to follow through on the countermeasures he proposed. Sanderson was delighted to see that the merits of the plan were no longer the chief subject of conversation: The most recent A3 reflecting the meaningful input and iterations of everyone was good. The argument for action spoke for itself.

4. Oscar Hammerstein II and Richard Rodgers, *The King and I*, 1956.

From Position-Based Authority to Pull-Based Authority

Lean management is neither a simple top-down nor bottom-up process. Rather, it is a dynamic system in which processes are well-defined, and individual responsibility is clear (and placed at the "lowest" possible level, where the work is taking place). As a result, responsibility and authority, which are generally assumed to be neatly bundled together, are revealed as separate and distinct.

Lean managers focus on responsibility and ownership, which means keying on "doing the right thing," as opposed to authority, which deals with who has the *right* to make certain decisions. As a result, decisions are made by a fundamentally different approach. The authority to make decisions is not established by hierarchy or titles. Rather, the owner of the A3, through the process of producing the dialogue, takes responsibility to *get decisions made.*

Responsibility ≠ Authority

This dynamic relies on the gemba-based approach to planning and problem-solving, which emphasizes that those who know the work are the right ones to participate in the conversation. Thus the responsible person uses the process of gathering facts and involving individuals to establish the authority needed to get the work done and the decision made.

Another counterintuitive aspect of A3 learning is that the process of coaxing agreement from key stakeholders becomes the means of gaining the authority needed for any plan or action. The conventional wisdom is that agreement is ordered by the person with the authority to command others into alignment. Agreement in a lean organization emerges from the inclusive process, which in turn produces authority. Essentially, authority is created by framing the issue properly and gaining agreement.

This process places great emphasis on generating sound, well-vetted proposals, rather than on making decisions from on-high. In essence, no one is telling anyone else what to do. Such a way of acting avoids much of the gridlock of centrally organized, top-down organizations. The lean company operates on a shared understanding of the desired corporate direction; and the workers are then free to explore the best possible real solutions to problems that they themselves know best.

"When we began this project, you didn't know anything about the document-translation process," he said with encouragement. "Now you're an expert. You were able to grasp the problem at a deep level—at the real root cause—because you put down your firefighter hat and became an impartial, objective investigator. It's time to turn this set of ideas into a plan and take it more formally to the organization.

"Now I need you to take off your investigator's hat and become an advocate," Sanderson uncharacteristically advised. "Among the various alternatives you have put together you must decide which countermeasures that you will propose and champion. You now know more about this issue than anyone else in the company. Both you and the company have invested to make you that expert. You must realize that clearly makes you the true problem owner—with the obligation to put forward the best possible recommendation. You cannot take a hands-off, laissez-faire approach going forward."

Sanderson paused for effect. Then he added, "Put yourself in the position of the company. What do you propose that Acme do?"

Porter considered this question and Sanderson's comments. He was relatively pleased with the current set of countermeasures, and so, taking all he'd written and rewritten, he focused on the few ideas in their simplest form. He was confident this latest A3 was best for the company (*see pages 84–85*).

This A3 would earn Porter the authority to go forward with his proposal. Sanderson noted this change with a bit of pride and even relief (unlike his reaction earlier in his career when letting go of details was difficult for him). Some aspects of lean managing, such as resisting the urge to jump in and solve his subordinates' problems, still felt counterintuitive. Yet he had become familiar, even comfortable with his role as sensei, asking questions instead of giving solutions. This was a matter of gaining more effective control by allowing his subordinate to learn through experience.

The basis for action was as clear as the A3 on his desk.

Key Questions

- Have you explored every reasonable alternative countermeasure?
- Have you produced viable alternatives based on productive conversations with everyone doing the work? With customers of the process? With stakeholders?
- Can you show how your proposed actions will address the root causes of the performance problems?
- Can you justify why your proposed actions are necessary?
- Have you continued to go to the gemba in gathering new information and countermeasures?

Porter's A3—Countermeasures for Acme

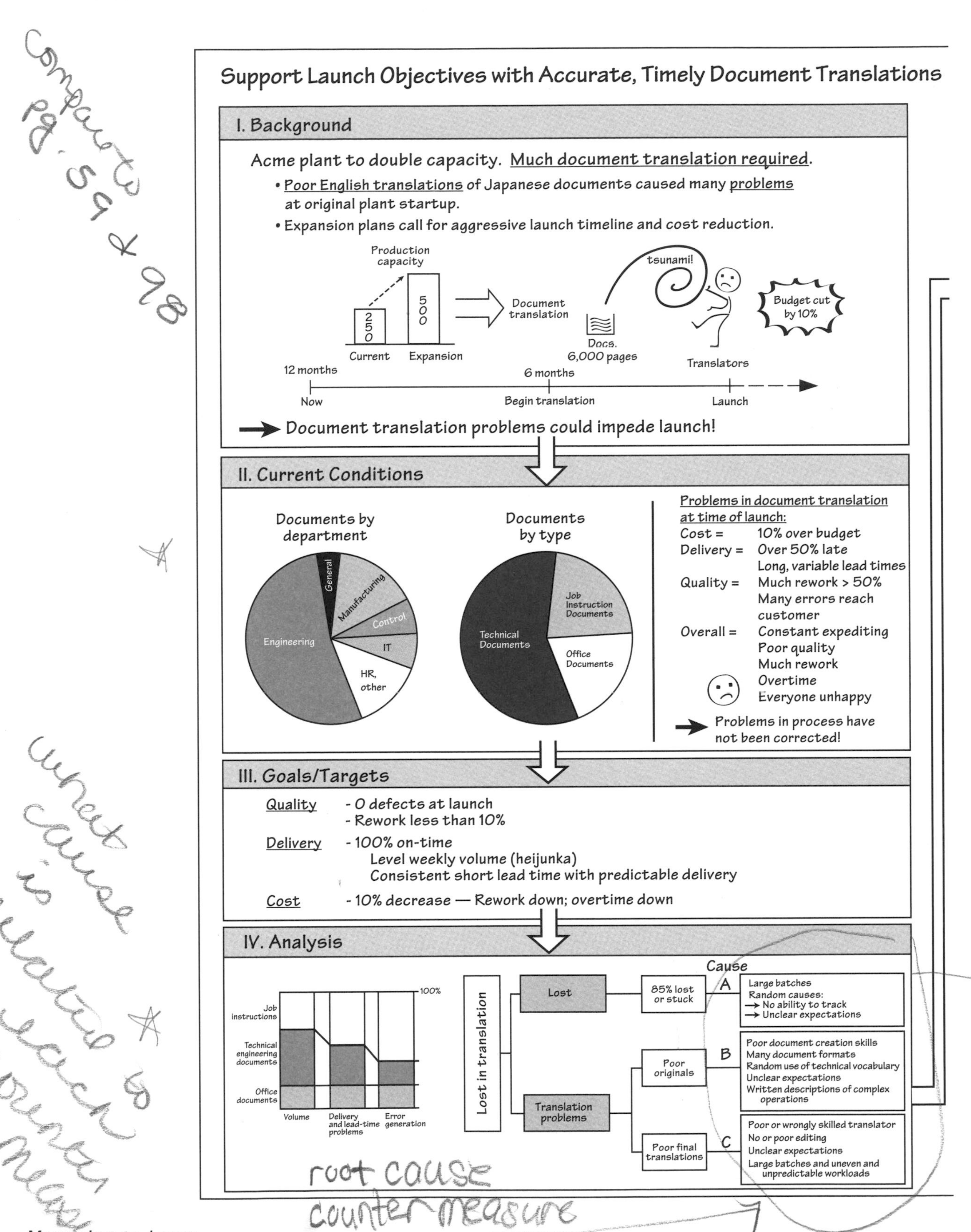

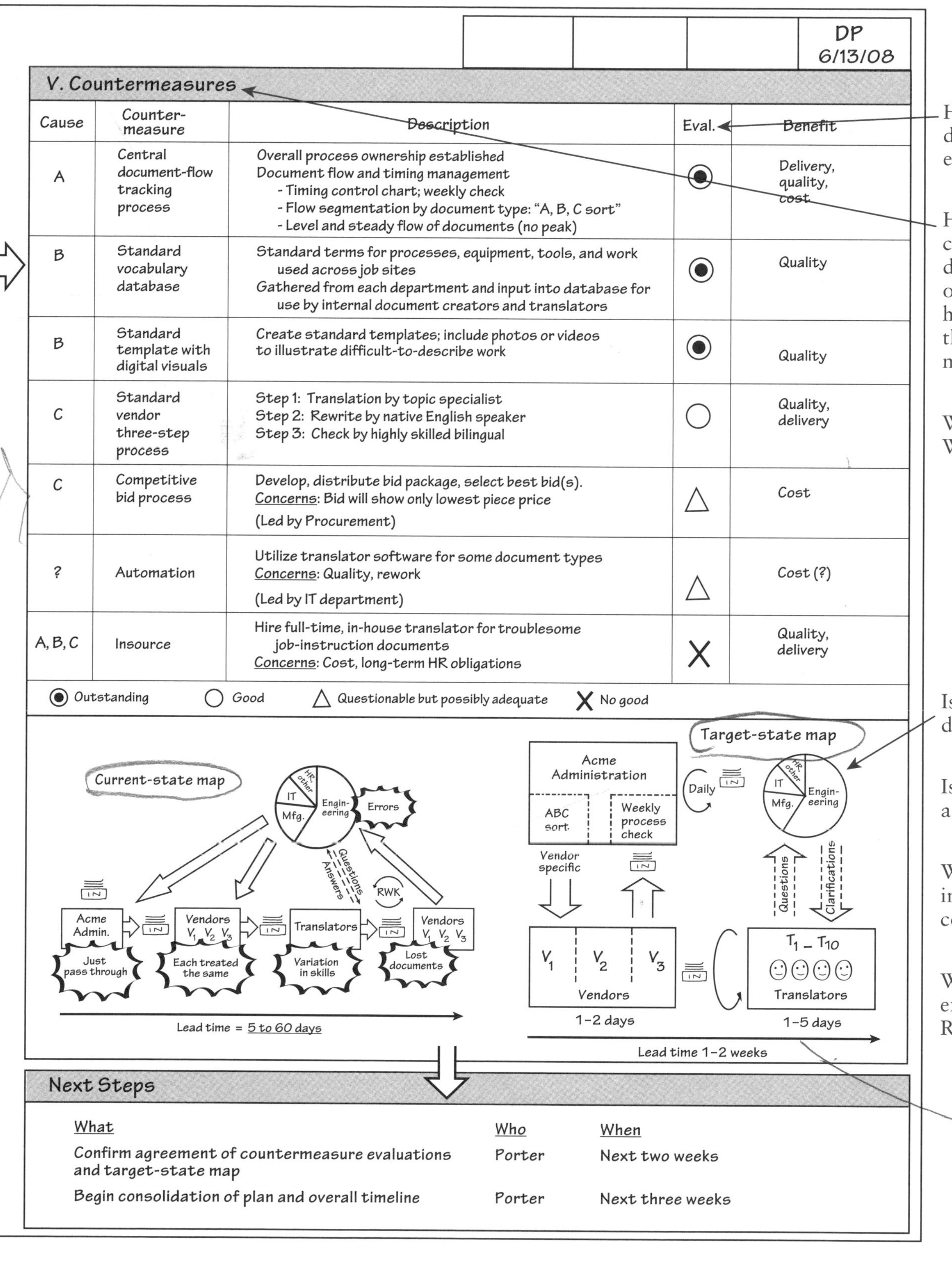

DP
6/13/08

V. Countermeasures

Cause	Counter-measure	Description	Eval.	Benefit
A	Central document-flow tracking process	Overall process ownership established Document flow and timing management - Timing control chart; weekly check - Flow segmentation by document type: "A, B, C sort" - Level and steady flow of documents (no peak)	◉	Delivery, quality, cost
B	Standard vocabulary database	Standard terms for processes, equipment, tools, and work used across job sites Gathered from each department and input into database for use by internal document creators and translators	◉	Quality
B	Standard template with digital visuals	Create standard templates; include photos or videos to illustrate difficult-to-describe work	◉	Quality
C	Standard vendor three-step process	Step 1: Translation by topic specialist Step 2: Rewrite by native English speaker Step 3: Check by highly skilled bilingual	○	Quality, delivery
C	Competitive bid process	Develop, distribute bid package, select best bid(s). Concerns: Bid will show only lowest piece price (Led by Procurement)	△	Cost
?	Automation	Utilize translator software for some document types Concerns: Quality, rework (Led by IT department)	△	Cost (?)
A, B, C	Insource	Hire full-time, in-house translator for troublesome job-instruction documents Concerns: Cost, long-term HR obligations	X	Quality, delivery

◉ Outstanding ○ Good △ Questionable but possibly adequate X No good

Next Steps

What	Who	When
Confirm agreement of countermeasure evaluations and target-state map	Porter	Next two weeks
Begin consolidation of plan and overall timeline	Porter	Next three weeks

How did you determine the evaluations?

How much consensus does the organization have around the countermeasure?

Who agrees? Who disagrees?

Is this doable?

Is there any risk?

What is the incremental cost?

What is the expected ROI?

Chapter 5
Plan and Followup—Pull-Based Authority

PDCA serves as the engine behind the A3 process. As Porter and his team test the proposed countermeasures, they use the PDCA (plan, do, check, act) cycle as a way of determining precisely how the plan will be implemented (who does what, when, and what mechanisms are in place to monitor this), and how to respond to what is —and isn't—working. They see how the learning cycle of PDCA is at the heart of the A3 process of producing operational learning.

Sanderson continues to use the A3 process as a means of creating agreement and organizational alignment. We see how Porter's evolving A3 report fits into Sanderson's array of challenges. And we also see how essential (and challenging) it is to continue using A3 thinking when things deviate from plan, which they are certain to do: "Plans are worthless. Planning is everything."[1]

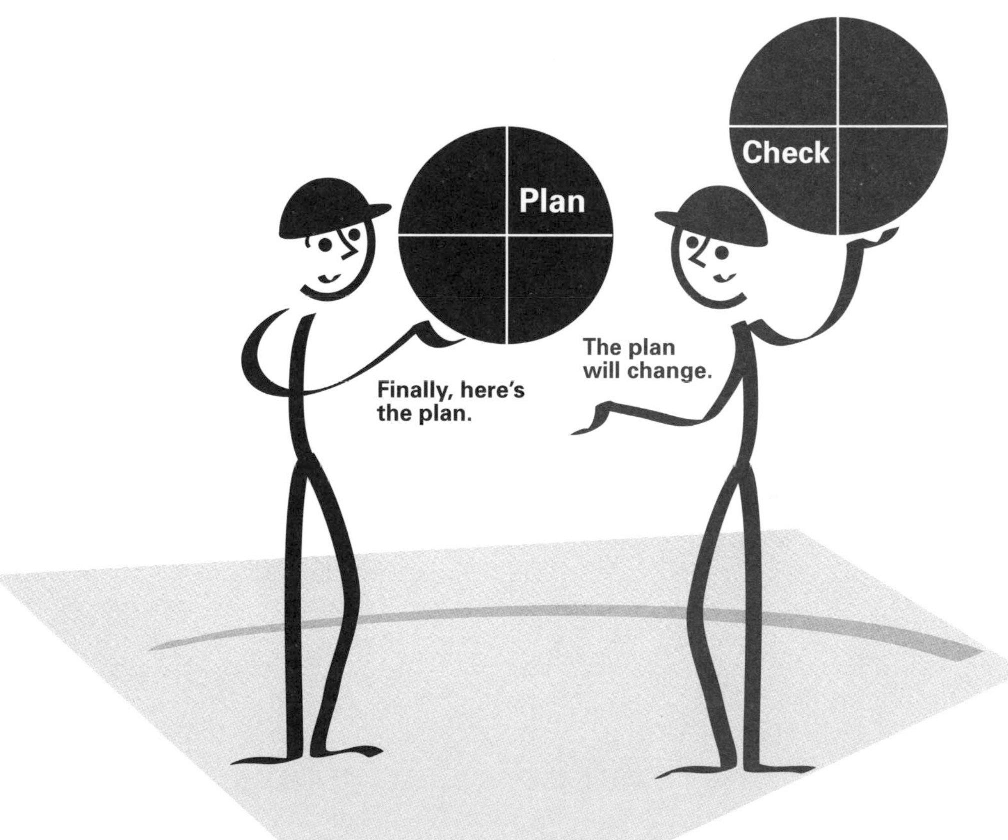

1. Dwight D. Eisenhower, 1957.

What's the Plan?

Porter stared at the A3 proposal on his desk. As Sanderson had told him, now it was time to formally take his proposal to the organization and see how the ideas would work, testing them out along the way.

Sanderson emphasized that the proposal was ready because the set of recommendations, though authored by Porter, was clearly produced in conjunction with the people doing the work. Of course some individuals were more involved in specific actions than others, but the main thing was that they had all seen and discussed the plan, with a clear hand in getting ideas on paper.

In addition to working at gaining approval for the countermeasures from myriad parties—and removing two ideas based on feedback from all—Porter had also gained their willingness to support the "what" and the "when." Various managers had promised that they'd free up resources to help. All that remained was the small matter of putting this plan into action.

In the *Plan* box of his A3 report, Porter scoped out the details of who would do what, how they would do this, when, and how the work would be monitored. For details and commitments, Porter created a Gantt chart to schedule and monitor the plan consistent with Acme's overall expansion plan (*see Acme's High-Level Plan—The Context on page 89*).

The Gantt chart specified outcomes, actions, and their duration, and it assigned responsibility for each action and set a timetable for when it would be completed and checked. Along the left-hand side he wrote a description of the tasks that would need to be accomplished as part of realizing the broader goal.

Plans and Planning

Sanderson laid a copy of Porter's A3 on his desktop. He studied it along with the A3s of the other dozen or so major projects he was involved with, all in various stages of planning or implementation.

The A3 reports on his desk covered a range of goals and themes; they addressed everything from short-term improvement projects to specific technical problems to broad organizational objectives. One report sought to reduce defects on a particular module; another targeted reduced injuries in stamping.

A few A3s on Sanderson's desk bore his name as owner. For example, he was the owner of proposals dealing with commonizing components and reducing parts inventory for the division, improving local community relations, and reducing the plant's total environmental impact.

For each of those, he had sought the same level of participation and input from all quarters that he asked of Porter. And he often had the same difficult discussions with his boss and the plant senior management committee.

His most important and challenging A3 was a report titled, "Expansion Excellence," for which he had many individual goals that were slowly moving forward. Porter's document-translation issue was one of these.

Acme's High-Level Plan—The Context

Acme Expansion Timetable

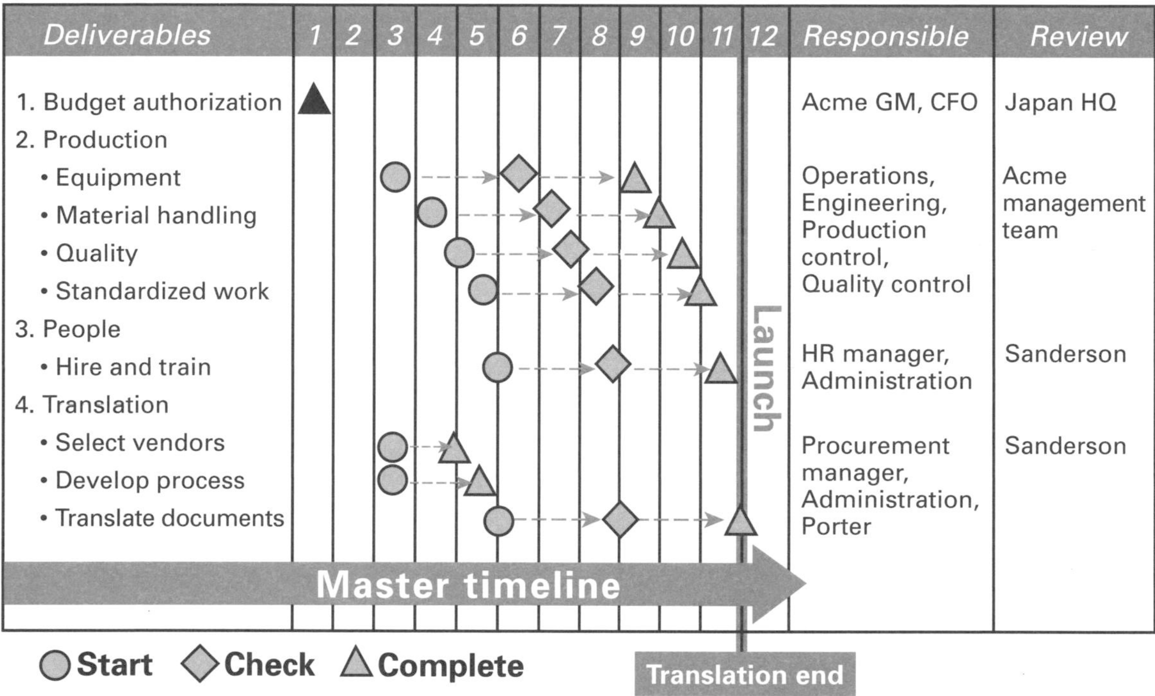

The full Gantt chart itself required an A3-sized sheet of paper. Porter summarized it for inclusion in the *Plan* section of the A3 report. As a simple chart, as with the overall A3 report, the value of a Gantt chart is in the usage, not the chart itself.

Porter knew, from experience, that a Gantt chart—or any other such plan—was above all a contract, a commitment to actually accomplish a specific set of goals by a specified time. So he was careful to base targets and deadlines on recommendations from the team.

Naturally this triggered yet another round of going to the gemba, in which Porter shopped around the latest version of his A3. Porter became Porter was on track with the translation-process effort, but other individuals working with other A3s were not gaining traction. For example, an A3 on "Startup Human Resources" for recruiting, hiring, and training new employees and supervisors for the expansion was stuck in neutral because the HR staffer assigned to the project was reticent to get out of her office and talk with shopfloor employees and supervisors in order to define criteria. Similarly, a report on capital-equipment requirements was behind because vendors didn't like the accustomed to revising the plan on the spot in response to each productive recommendation.

For example, Carter had insights into how each of the three roles in the three-step translation process would test the new standard process for editing and transmitting the documents. The Japanese technical writer would create a preliminary glossary of the technical terms that are most often used.

Additionally, the Japanese-to-English translator and the bilingual engineer would need to create working glossaries for the most basic terms, with deeper standardization emerging as the new system was put into use. Finally, Carter volunteered to coordinate the total flow of work for technical documents.

With each key individual, Porter reviewed responsibilities for each deliverable, confirmed target dates, and noted who would review them. It was the target dates that generated the greatest debate. "go to the gemba" approach (i.e., "Do you really need to see how this works? Can't you just try it and then let us adapt it for you?"); nor did they like the special requirements the expansion plant's new processes required ("This is good enough for our other customers—just look at our quality awards.").

Sanderson had no shortage of headaches. All the more reason that it was important for him to help Porter succeed in the next phase of the document-translation project.

As the expansion launch date approached, timing and all its aspects and in all things were becoming increasingly critical. Sanderson recalled an important lesson from one of his Acme mentors: "One of the most

A3 revisions at the gemba

Timing had been one of the biggest problems during document translation for the initial plant startup. Not only did many documents miss their specific target dates, but rework continued well past the launch. Furthermore, the work began so early that the entire process had seemed to go on forever. After much discussion with all parties, Porter's recommendation entailed a radically different timing schedule (*see page* 92): document-translation work starting later, ramping up much more quickly, and leveling the work load to eliminate the huge peak in work load that occurred before.

Porter prepared to share his plan with Sanderson. They had been testing parts of the proposal all along. By now everyone had had the opportunity to review it in its entirety. And Porter realized that the current version of the plan was not only more granular in detail and contained countermeasures that directly addressed problems, but it felt more doable.

Walking the gemba—indeed the many gembas of where individuals did the work—had involved more conflict, resistance, and surprises than he could have expected. But as he readied himself for Sanderson's tough reading of the plan, he felt confident that these measures were powerful, and that all individuals involved, through sharing their direct knowledge of the work, would fully support the proposal.

Finally, after so much preparation, Porter believed that the plan was ready to be tested.

important skills of any manager is creating deadlines. No assignment is complete, no proposal actionable until target dates have been established. Sometimes simply establishing a cadence of return visits to check on progress can in itself be powerful—Toyota leaders often finish operations reviews with the phrase, "I'll be back in two weeks!"[1]

It is important, however, that the deadlines *feel real*, not arbitrary, even if they sometimes are somewhat discretionary. In this case the launch date was looming, making all subordinate target dates real and imminent.

I'll be back in two weeks!

1. Seiji Yamamoto in *Toyota Kuchiguse* (Common expressions of Toyota Leaders") by OJT Solutions (Tokyo: Chukei Shuppan, 2006).

Porter's Radically Different Timing and Workload Schedule—Level and Steady

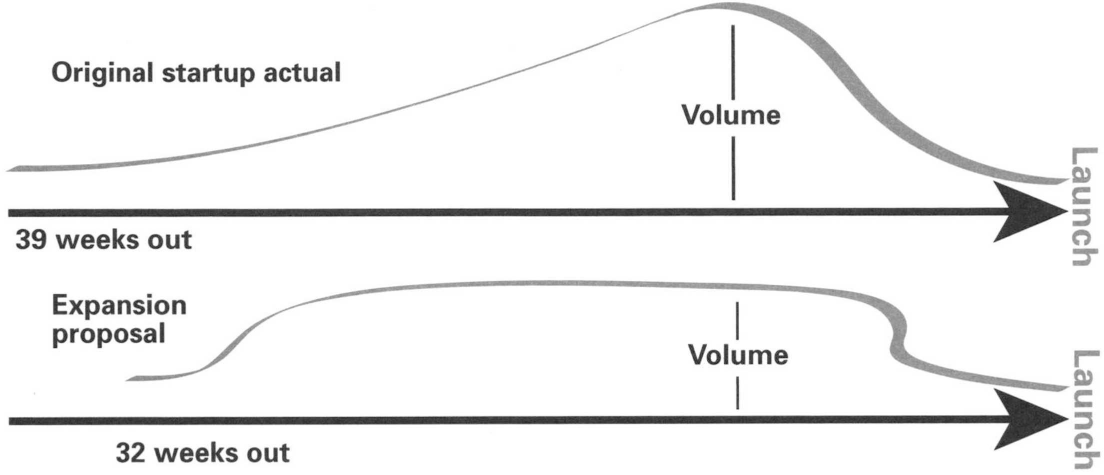

Just-In-Time Decision-Making

In companies whose thinking is informed by the A3 process, managers at every level make the right decision only *when it is exactly the right time to do so*. Choosing a solution too early can easily lock in the wrong choice. That's because premature solutions often reflect political agendas, impulsive analysis, or poor judgment. They rarely reflect the shared understanding or agreement necessary for successful execution. Nor do they have sufficient facts or engaged consensus to succeed.

A3 thinking triggers decision-making at the right time by focusing the debate on the facts at hand, involving the right participation through dialogue, and enabling the choice to be made only when all the options have been assessed by the key players. This process grants the authority to make the decision to the person who has the responsibility to do so: the owner of the report.

The A3 helps the manager prevent people from making decisions too quickly.

No Problem is Problem

"Now," said Sanderson, "tell me how you plan to keep moving forward on this project. How can you share what your team has learned from all this? And who's going to make sure that the new process continues to work as intended?"

"Well, I'm glad you asked," Porter replied. He had anticipated this question, and had prepared a management review process to ensure everything was working smoothly as viewed by each person at each step through the process: first the customers, then the workers, and finally Porter and all those supporting the process.

Porter outlined his process for monitoring progress. "We are ensuring that people at each step along the way know the preceding and following steps and have quick, continual feedback regarding timing and quality. In addition, to evaluate overall system performance and cost, we will compile a running analysis and make it available to team leaders of each major process, the factory, the translation company, and management at our mother plant in Japan."

Sanderson was quiet for some time as he reviewed this set of measures on paper. They were detailed, precise, and focused on the metrics of success as originally defined. Then he looked up and said: "Great! Now let's talk about what kinds of things could go wrong."

"Well, something could always go wrong," Porter replied. "But I believe we've covered most things pretty well."

Porter was unsure. "It feels strange to list everything that can go wrong at the end of the plan. If there are problems we can foresee, why don't we just deal with them in the plan to begin with? And

Questioning Minds

Sanderson had one overarching theme for every interaction with his staff: "Create reflective problem-solvers." And at one time he had produced his own A3 report as a means of achieving this goal, recalling his supervisor's words when they were preparing for the original plant startup: "We need to produce good people before we can produce good products."

Porter's growth reflected progress on this A3, freeing Sanderson to focus on other staff members, some of whom were still struggling. And when they struggled, Sanderson struggled.

Sanderson could envision any number of potential results from the new way of working. He considered the ramifications to the company, the suppliers, the customers, and even to external concerns such as public relations and regulatory issues.

For example, as a result of Porter's work, Sanderson had discovered that the new plans relied on the outsourcing of several key functions—such as translating—more than he had realized. As a result, it was vulnerable to production lapses if the various vendors could not deliver.

One of the more counterintuitive aspects Sanderson had found about A3 management was the radically different attitude that one needed to develop toward finding problems.

besides, won't listing all the potential flaws and abnormalities insult the team members who are now proud that they are putting forth their best?"

"This takes nothing away from the people," replied Sanderson. "They may react defensively —but your job is to show that asking what might go wrong is supportive. You are acknowledging that their approach has merited implementation. And now you are refocusing a lens forward rather than backward. You are doing no more than asking 'what if' questions similar to those used seeking alternative countermeasures. We want to anticipate so we can help ensure that the plan succeeds."

Acknowledging just how far Porter had come as a manager, Sanderson discussed his own role and the role of corporate leadership. "Our senior management team knows that plans are things that change," Sanderson said. "This particular A3 plan is just one stop along the way, one piece of an overall plan for our expansion, which in turn is part of the company's overall strategic plan. Each individual plan or proposal is a building block for an architecture that will evolve forever in the face of changing conditions."

Sanderson paused and continued: "Your job is to foresee problems and the barriers that might crop up to prevent this plan from succeeding. Help your team become comfortable with looking forward and think of how you can focus their attention on opportunities for learning and improvement."

Porter went back to his team. This was difficult for him; he felt good about the entire process, and was reluctant to talk about negatives. Nonetheless, he saw this as a way to grow as a manager, and help his team prepare. He started an inquisitive

A born detail-person, Sanderson *hated* to make mistakes. He had grown up thinking of this as a positive trait that was key to the success he had enjoyed early in his career.

But as he gained broader responsibility and tried to project onto his staff his own attitude toward problems, he found that his staff was reluctant to bring problems forward. This pattern of hiding problems, he learned from his mentor, was a much bigger problem than the problem itself.

dialogue about what could go wrong—trying to reinforce his belief that by nature of implementing the plan, the plan was good and the team was making progress. This back-and-forth with team members helped him come up with new set of followup procedures that would address both positive and negative outcomes.

Porter and his team found two potential pitfalls:

- This system would increase the number of handoffs between individuals in some cases, increasing the potential for delays, drops, or other lapses in flow.
- This plan would add a new burden, at least in the beginning, for Acme people who must develop, deliver, and undergo training and follow a new process.

Porter realized it was time to proceed. He had earned the authorization to go forward. He was pleased. Sanderson had initialed his A3 (*see Porter's Authorized A3 on pages 98–99*).

Celebrate Mistakes

From:
Mistakes are bad—hide them.

To:
Mistakes happen—celebrate finding them.

PDCA

PDCA (plan, do, check, act/adjust/action) is a management cycle based on the scientific method of proposing a change in a process, implementing the change, monitoring and measuring the results, and taking appropriate action. It also is known as the "Deming Cycle" or "Deming Wheel" after W. Edwards Deming, who introduced the concept in Japan in the 1950s in a simpler form and refined it over the following decades. The PDCA process as a system for continuous improvement has been studied and modified by many, and similar management or decision cycles have emerged over the years: LAMDA (look, ask, model, discuss, act), an acronym for Al Ward's "cycle of knowledge creation," and OODA (observe, orient, decide, act), a decision cycle that was developed by military strategist John Boyd.

The PDCA cycle has four stages:

1. *Plan*: Determine the problems with the current conditions, goals for a process, and needed changes to achieve them with actions and subgoals. *Think "hypothesis."*
2. *Do*: Give the changes or the new process a try. *Think "experiment, trial."*
3. *Check*: Evaluate the results. Ask what was learned. *Think "study and reflect."*
4. *Act*: Incorporate the learning into the new process. Standardize and stabilize the change and begin again. *Think "adjust and standardize."*

The power of PDCA is fully realized within the systematic approach of A3 thinking. On one level, A3 does no more than operationalize the PDCA process by capturing what you are going to do, how you are going to check on it, and how you are going to make adjustments. Yet on a broader level, the actual use of the A3 ensures that PDCA occurs as a learning process. As a question, suggestion, and a way of generating productive conversation, the A3 ensures that the PDCA process enables and captures operational learning. A3 thinking can be seen as a way of ensuring that the PDCA process converts several broad and abstract managerial goals into real results and "deep organizational capability" at the same time.[2]

The PDCA cycle

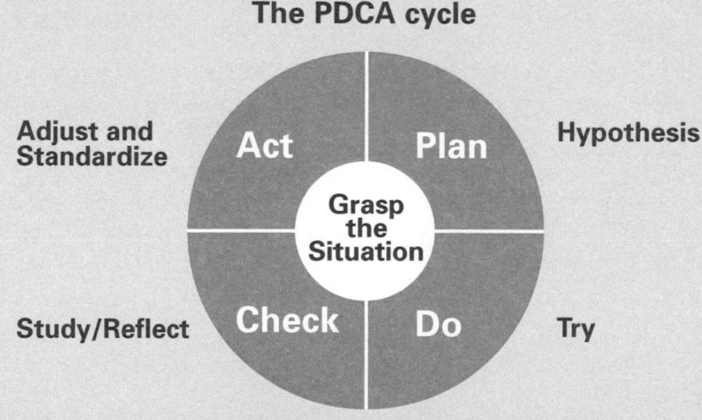

From pDpD (try, fail, try, fail) to PDCA cycle

2. Takahiro Fujimoto, *Competing to Be Really, Really Good* (Tokyo: International House of Japan, 2007).

Key Questions

- Has problem-solving shifted from quick fixes to root-cause counter-measures?
- Does the current A3 reflect the input of the key people involved with the work? Do counter-measures have support?
- Do you see where your A3 (and the work it encompasses) fits into the A3s of colleagues below and above you (and their work)?
- Has the A3 continued to evolve through constant iteration as a result of experimenting with the initially proposed countermeasures?
- Are you using the PDCA cycle to implement the plan—and to gather knowledge from experiments?

Porter's Authorized A3

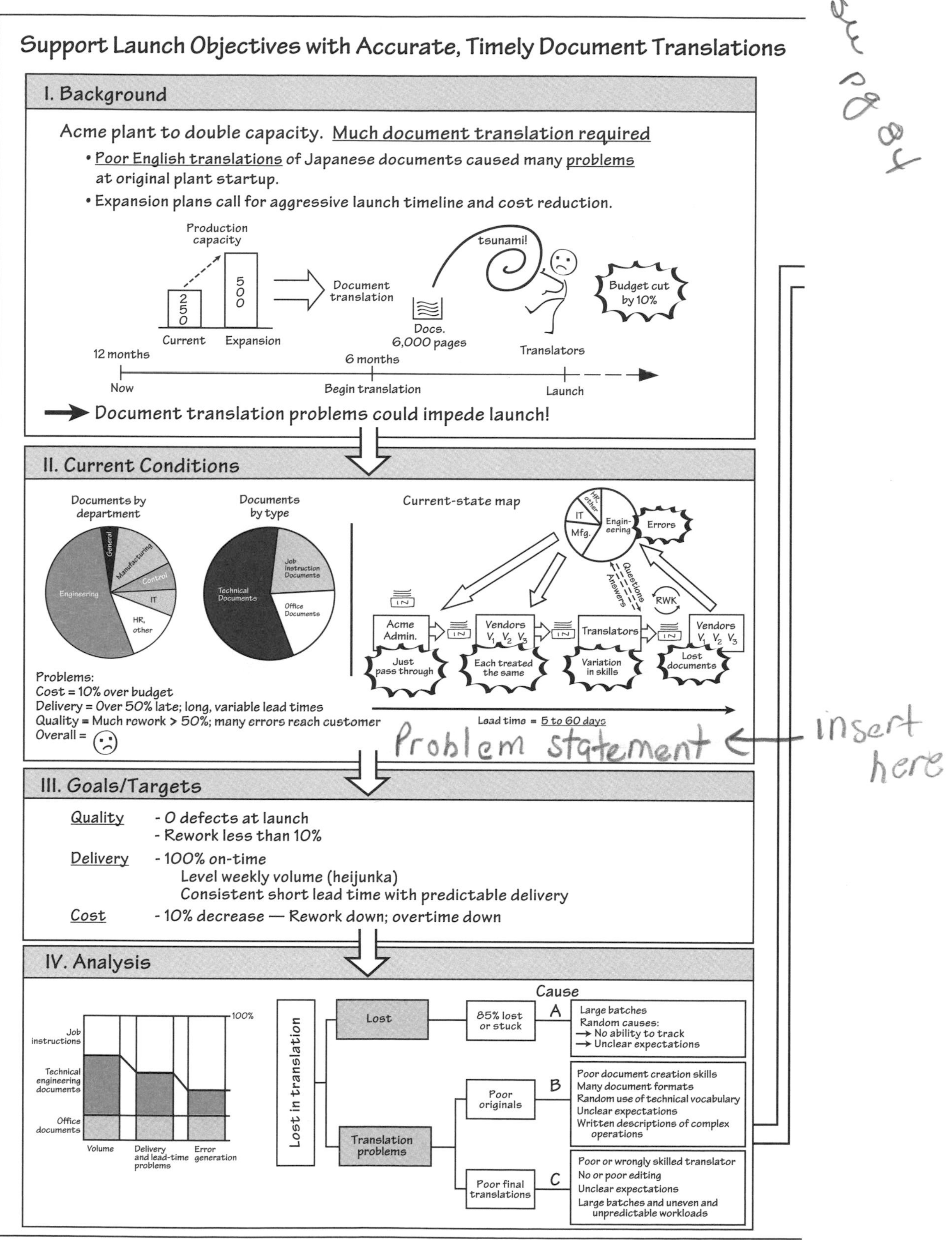

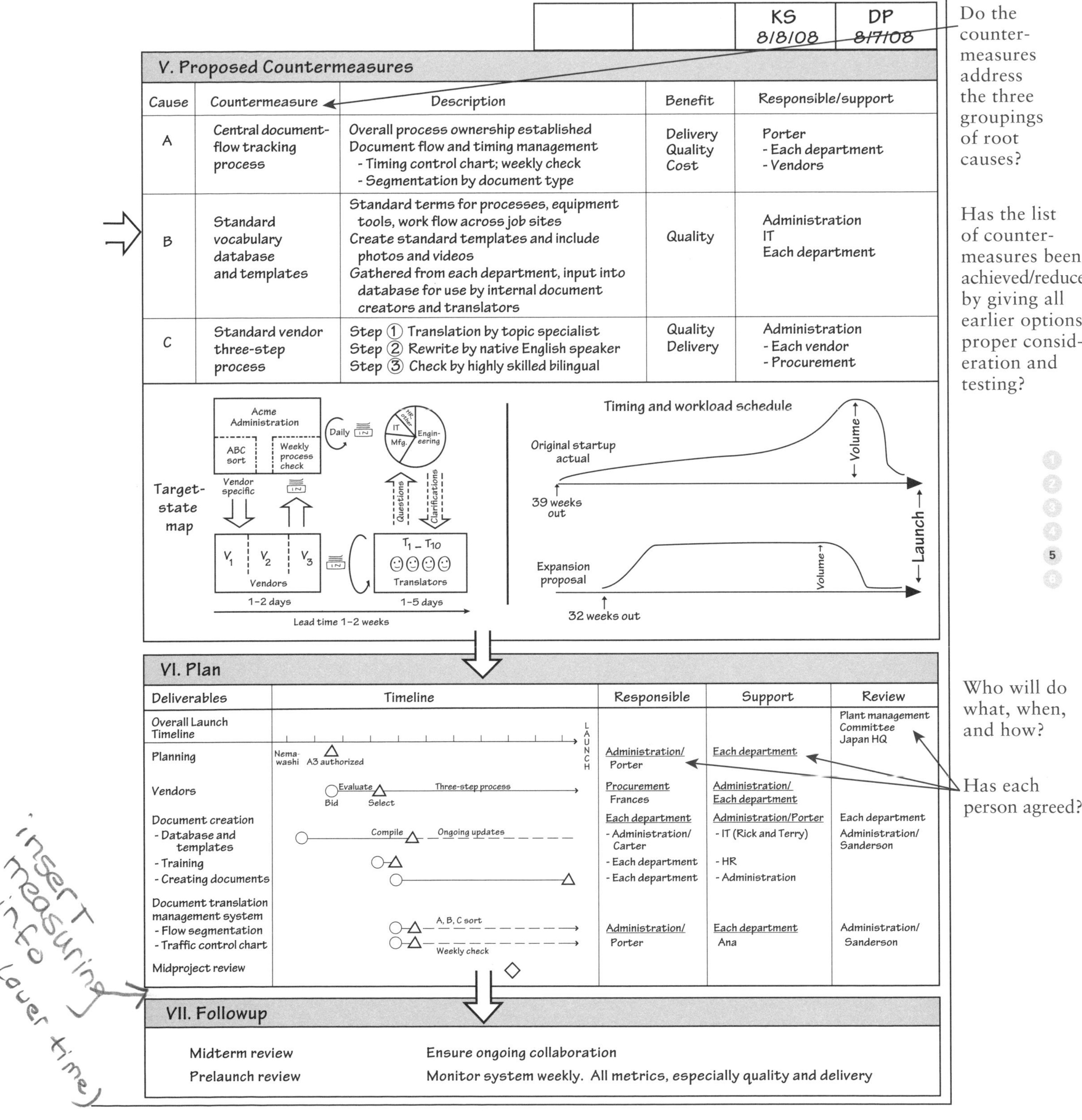

		KS 8/8/08	DP 8/7/08

Do the countermeasures address the three groupings of root causes?

Has the list of countermeasures been achieved/reduced by giving all earlier options proper consideration and testing?

V. Proposed Countermeasures

Cause	Countermeasure	Description	Benefit	Responsible/support
A	Central document-flow tracking process	Overall process ownership established Document flow and timing management - Timing control chart; weekly check - Segmentation by document type	Delivery Quality Cost	Porter - Each department - Vendors
B	Standard vocabulary database and templates	Standard terms for processes, equipment tools, work flow across job sites Create standard templates and include photos and videos Gathered from each department, input into database for use by internal document creators and translators	Quality	Administration IT Each department
C	Standard vendor three-step process	Step ① Translation by topic specialist Step ② Rewrite by native English speaker Step ③ Check by highly skilled bilingual	Quality Delivery	Administration - Each vendor - Procurement

VI. Plan

Who will do what, when, and how?

Deliverables	Timeline	Responsible	Support	Review
Overall Launch Timeline	LAUNCH			Plant management Committee Japan HQ
Planning	Nemawashi; A3 authorized	Administration/ Porter	Each department	
Vendors	Bid; Evaluate; Select; Three-step process	Procurement Frances	Administration/ Each department	
Document creation		Each department	Administration/Porter	Each department
- Database and templates	Compile; Ongoing updates	- Administration/ Carter	- IT (Rick and Terry)	Administration/ Sanderson
- Training		- Each department	- HR	
- Creating documents		- Each department	- Administration	
Document translation management system		Administration/ Porter	Each department Ana	Administration/ Sanderson
- Flow segmentation	A, B, C sort			
- Traffic control chart	Weekly check			
Midproject review	◇			

Has each person agreed?

insert measuring info (over time)

VII. Followup

Midterm review	Ensure ongoing collaboration
Prelaunch review	Monitor system weekly. All metrics, especially quality and delivery

1 2 3 4 5 6

Chapter 6
Perpetual PDCA—Developing A3 Thinkers

Porter learns that developing and implementing effective countermeasures is not the end of the process. Now that the original goals have been addressed, his role is to share what has been learned, standardize and communicate key practices, implement a system for reviewing the work, and apply a fresh eye toward continued improvements. This work will not only address mechanical or process matters, but must be guided by the primary goal of teaching every individual a shared way of thinking and working, one that can cascade down to the lowest level of employee and work across the entire company.

Meanwhile, Sanderson considers how to incorporate the results of this project into broader organizational goals and into ongoing projects. He assesses how well Acme's A3 thinking marries strategy and execution—how broad goals are tested out in real settings by reflective problem-solvers—and how the knowledge that is eventually captured through the linked process of policy deployment helps generate new and better strategy.

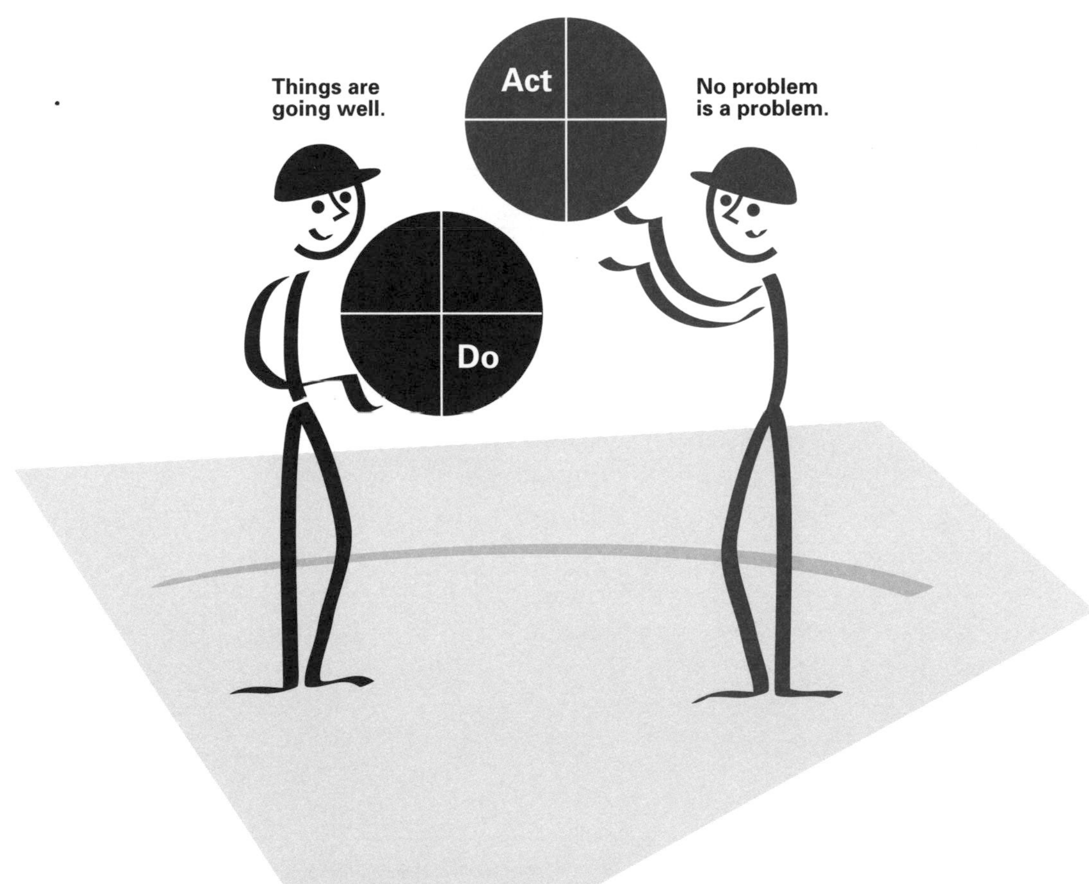

A3 Management

It had been almost three months since the bulk of the document translation for the expansion project had begun. It was almost time for the three-month review. Porter was a bit nervous about it, but confident in the progress being made.

One of the biggest successes involved the job instruction translations, which had been such a big concern in the past. The new improved process, with the standard template and visual images to show the work, proved to be extremely popular with the workers on the plant floor. The translated job instruction documents were only drafts, intended to serve as the beginning point for the plant floor operators to take ownership, to even rewrite them as they used them to solve problems when they had trouble in maintaining their standard work and to raise the level of performance through kaizen. Acme managers were delighted to see that the workers were already using the new job instruction documents to conduct kaizen experiments on the actual work in the Acme shops. The work described by some of the documents had already been greatly improved, even prior to the pending launch.

But, of course, there were also many problems. One major issue was that the handoffs were not going as smoothly as hoped. In particular, some translators would make changes up to the last minute—often they would process difficult documents by dropping in new terms on the fly, producing confusion down the line. Other translators would revert to old behavior and sit on work-in-process. But overall the changes were yielding most of the savings and quality improvements for which Porter had hoped.

Managing the Means

Sanderson was tempted to accept Porter's preliminary findings, slot in new projected results into his A3 report, and pass this along to his boss as a sign of progress in the broader plant expansion goals. Yet he held off. Now more than ever, he needed to lead Porter and his team by coaching, mentoring, and, above all, acting in the same hands-on approach he needed them to develop.

He needed to keep Porter focused on applying A3 thinking during this tactical phase. It was always tempting to slip into satisfaction from seeing quick fixes emerge out of the Five Whys process. Yet enduring change resulted from applying A3 thinking to *implementing* the countermeasures of a properly framed plan.

Sure, he could share a few thoughts on how to manage—but the real lessons would still come from focusing on the pragmatic details of making this plan work. Porter needed to keep working to "lower the water," as lean veterans would say. According to this parable, the more waste that was identified and removed, the easier it should be to see even more waste lurking below the surface. Now, how would he break up rocks that emerged? Could there be a better way? And, if so, how would it be realized?

Porter and Sanderson met to discuss the challenge Porter was having getting individuals to accept responsibility for problems. Porter found himself complaining about the attitude he was observing in others.

Sanderson encouraged Porter to, "Focus on the timing and deliverables of your plan as much as the action items. Use them as reference points to tell you how things are working."

"But what if people aren't hitting their marks?" Porter asked. "Shouldn't people do what they say? After all, we've all come up with what should be achievable goals. They agreed to the plan, they should follow it."

Sanderson paused, considering how to get his point across. "When things deviate from plan—as they almost certainly will—your responsibility is not to just ask if people did their jobs or to harass them until they do. Your role is to keep everyone focused on *why* things went wrong—and just as importantly, why they went right. It's not just about the people, it's also about the process. Remember, that is why you've established a *Followup* process—to follow up."

Porter kept Sanderson's advice in mind as he returned to the gemba to investigate why people continued to make so many last-minute changes. Importantly, he had asked some team members to take a piece of the overall process and develop their own A3s on how to improve it going forward. "Focus on the process; focus on the work," he told himself and others.

Porter found that this approach led to fewer turf battles than he anticipated (but it increasingly required that he fall back on characteristics he'd seen Sanderson exhibit with him only weeks

Regardless of progress to date and regardless of which part of the process they were in, Sanderson knew that internalizing A3 thinking should be the focal point. Constant improvement of the technical mastery of the format or the countermeasure at hand was essential but secondary. For tomorrow there would be other, completely different issues, projects, and opportunities that needed A3 thinking. The more cycles of reflection and learning, the better it is for the individual and for the organization.

Porter had come a long way, and Sanderson took a measure of pride in his growth. Yet they still had far to go. Porter's biggest problem remained his impulse to jump ahead to conclusions or actions. After several improvement cycles, he would feel as though his work was done.

Sanderson knew that falling back on management by auto-pilot would undo many of the gains already achieved, and would certainly undermine people's capacity to continue learning.

Avoiding the natural impulse to consider even significant progress sufficient was a temptation for Sanderson himself. Above all he needed to be diligent about avoiding complacency in his role as a leader.

He understood leadership to mean one primary mission. His objective was to get people to think and take before). Since managers and departments had either offered or signed off on the countermeasures and committed resources, the turf battles had become nearly a nonissue. The plan was transparent to all. Everyone had agreed upfront on overall goals, major changes, and action items, and their agreement *was made visible for all to see*. Everyone could see how their role was dependent on others producing their deliverables in a timely manner. It was not exactly a well-oiled machine yet, but good teamwork had developed naturally as the plan was rolled out.

Porter and the team (a virtual "team," since they all resided in separate organizational as well as geographical locations) continued to drill down in their investigation. At first, as a way of improving performance, they created and introduced a timing chart to show where each document was in the process, highlighting anything that was stuck in the pipeline. This immediately helped illuminate where specific documents were, and, through color-coding, enabled anyone to show when one document was high-priority.

One particular exchange stuck out in Porter's mind. It reminded him that the people doing the work were likely to present the most effective countermeasures (but not always). In discussing the latest shortcomings of the trial run with a translator, Porter sought input on how to revise the process. He asked Yoshi, one of the most experienced translators, to develop an A3 around this issue. She was the most resistant to every change Porter had suggested, and he was expecting conflict.

initiative. Managing, he had learned, was all about thinking—developing the right way of approaching a problem. Leading was a matter of getting other people to think.[1] His greatest challenge remained finding ways to get other people to take responsibility and initiative.

For that, he would continue with the same approach at the heart of A3 thinking: asking questions. But his focus now was on setting challenging expectations and getting Porter to keep challenging to reach new targets. He focused on how to coach Porter following the planned three-month review.

Sanderson needed Porter to ensure that the various parts of the organization were truly aligned, in agreement with the plan as it was put into action. Since Porter was leading this effort as a "chief engineer"—with no real authority over any of the players and no direct reports—he would have to lead by securing commitment, not by seeking compliance.

The only authority he has is that which he earned through the A3 process: pull-based authority.

1. From an unpublished paper by David Verble, former manager of organizational development and management training for Toyota's North American manufacturing organization.

Gradually Yoshi became engaged in improving the process—not a source of conflict—and jumped in with ideas. She created an A3 that clearly described the problem as one of varying stages of translation complexity, and then proposed a countermeasure to reduce complexity. "How about separating the work into two streams—simple and complex—and then dealing with each of the streams on a simple first-in, first-out basis?" she asked, pointing to her A3. She suggested a small trial to test the idea.

Porter and His 'Virtual Team'

As the work proceeded, delays and other problems naturally continued to crop up. Porter and his team continued to design new A3s analyzing the sources of particular delays—and occasionally their observation led them to a "just do it" when the root cause was clear and the countermeasure obvious. As a result of these A3 reports, and the discoveries produced by the back-and-forth conversation with the authors (just as Sanderson had worked with Porter), Porter and the team were able to implement and test countermeasures to the problems of getting the documents moving smoothly.

Porter was pleased with the overall results. The three-step translation process was proving to be effective in tracking errors and speeding up the process. And even though it was still a work-in-progress, the standardized glossary already had dramatically lowered the number of errors in documents.

Kanban Democracy

One of the greatest challenges for managers in this situation is to continue to lead and exercise responsibility in a manner tied to the A3 process.

Sanderson recalled that a true lean organization operates as what Toyota pioneer Taiichi Ohno called a "kanban democracy"[2] where authority is pulled to where it is needed when it is needed: on-demand, just-in-time, pull-based authority. A3s establish a set of clearly agreed-upon rules that generate a remarkably egalitarian organization. People step up to lead, manage, and take action when they have proven that it is the right course.

Porter would need to learn that exercising authority, like making a decision, was a delicate function that

2. Setsuo Mito, *An Album of a Management Revolution*, (Tokyo: Seiryu Shuppan, 2007).

The project of developing the standard vocabulary was leading to additional ideas and enthusiasm as everyone began to realize the potential of the change. The translators had already compiled a substantial list of key definitions they encountered in their work—a new idea—and had created a shared online space for them to post and review this resource, making it possible to gradually grow this vocabulary into a widely shared and commonly understood resource.

Porter met with Sanderson and reflected on the project. "So tell me how things are going," said Sanderson, looking for some insights prior to the formal three-month review.

"Well, it looks good on paper, but not everything is going exactly according to plan," Porter said.

"Plans are things that change," replied Sanderson. "What's going wrong?"

"Well," Porter continued, "as you know, putting together the glossary of standard vocabulary has proved to be more difficult than we thought. We are getting through that, but it turns out some of the shop rats don't want to use it."

Sanderson pressed for clarification, "What do you mean, they 'don't want to use it'?"

"We gave them the glossary and training three weeks ago, but they still don't follow the standard work."

Sanderson asked, "Do you know why they don't follow it? Have you asked them why they can't follow the standardized work?"

Porter replied, "Not in those terms. Yes of course, I'll ask them. Why not?"

Sanderson said, "Great. I'm anxious to hear how it goes. When can we meet next?"

could be exercised only when the situation dictated it—and not as a function of title or mindset. The A3 process would continue to guide him when it came to these junctures, forcing him or any other individual to meet the burden of proof to justify why they need to be able to decide. The A3 would serve as the basis for legitimatizing their plan and providing authorization to move forward.

Process rules, thought Sanderson. That's why official jobs and job titles in a lean organization sometimes appear to be in flux. One of the toughest challenges for A3 newcomers concerns their official job title vs. the actual work they are expected to do.

As Porter's success enabled Acme to reallocate resources, he and others would need to define their job by what they did rather than by formal titles. This was tough for people who sought clearly delineated areas of authority and well-guarded territories of control.

Yet as work improvements eliminate waste, or muda, in all its forms, then individuals must define their job responsibilities to match the new work. They can continually use the A3 process as a means of taking responsibility and gaining authority to do the work.

Pull-Based Authority

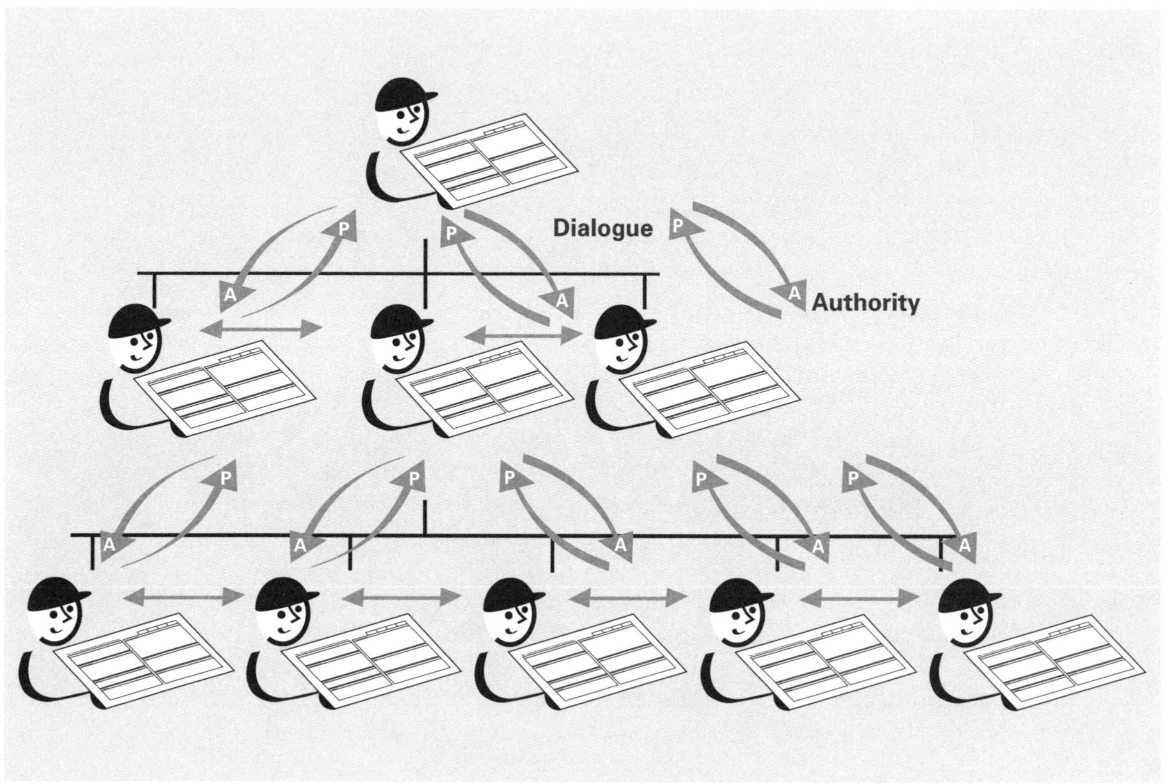

Each person at each level has clear responsibility and ownership, using the A3 for pull-based authority, getting the authority needed when needed.

6

> *Authority is pulled to where it is needed when it is needed: on-demand, just-in-time, pull-based authority.*

Mini-Shusa

One of the engines behind Toyota's successful managerial system is the role of the shusa, or product chief engineer. "Shusa" is a general word for a rank within many Japanese corporate hierarchies that at Toyota refers to an individual with broad responsibility for setting the vision and assuring the successful delivery of a product or project. Toyota's product development shusa does not directly control the resources required for success of the project or product for which he has broad responsibility. In Toyota, the shusa in the product development environment leads and coordinates all the processes and resources needed to deliver products for which he or she is responsible: to set and attain market-share goals, to solve complex organizational issues, etc.

Thorough implementation of the A3 management process can essentially convert a functional manager into a "mini-shusa." They must assume ownership of their project and deliver value to the customer horizontally across functions by integrating functions and processes that might otherwise operate vertically as silos (by hierarchy, function, or department).[3]

Mike Masaki, former president of the Toyota Technical Center USA, stated that any A3 proposal requires the owner's "omoi-ire"—the owner's own original thinking, to make it his own. Without it, the owner is just a caretaker of others' ideas, not a true owner, advocating and even fighting for his own ideas.

3. For a related concept, see the "mini-company" concept in: Kiyoshi Suzaki, *Results From the Heart* (New York: Free Press, 2002).

Reflections

Porter prepared for the three-month review, chaired by Sanderson and which would include the translation team, customers, stakeholders—all those touching the process. He and the translation team reflected on what they had learned. Beyond technical lessons, his goal was to test how well each of the participants had learned the A3 way of thinking, learning, and solving problems together.

Porter remembered one comment he had heard earlier about A3 reports: *The ultimate goal is not just to solve the problem at hand—but to make the process of problem-solving transparent and teachable in order to create an organization populated with problem-solvers.*

For the three-month review, Porter established "reflection in terms of people development" as the final item on the agenda, and pursued several key questions with the team:

- How well did people do in working through their assignments?
- Was learning being shared as the work progressed?
- Were there failures in actions or thinking that Porter as project owner needs to address the next time?
- Was the work proving easier or more difficult? Conversely, is a greater challenge called for?

These questions were not teed up to blame anyone; everybody understood that their goal was to find opportunities to improve (*see Porter's Review Agenda pages 112–113*).

The People Problem

Sanderson looked over all of the ongoing A3s he was overseeing, assessing the implications of Porter's program within the framework of greater goals he faced. As he pondered how Porter could support him, he recalled the saying, "You can delegate authority, but you can never delegate responsibility."[4] Porter had earned the authority to move forward, having stepped up and taken responsibility to rally the organization around his plan. Now, Sanderson's own responsibility would need to change.

This was an interesting problem for Sanderson, and he prepared an A3 report addressing the challenge. And before sharing this with his boss, he asked Porter to provide input on the facts he used in his own analysis of current conditions. He also sought Porter's opinion about other A3s sitting on his desk. For example, should an A3 on expansion staffing address the need for possibly hiring another bilingual engineer?

His work with Porter had been a good test of his own coaching skills. While tiring at times, it was not nearly as exhausting as telling Porter and others what to do or trying to firefight his way through these issues and problems. He felt confident that he could now rely on Porter and others for accurate data and problem-solving.

4. Jason Santamaria, Vincent Martino, and Eric K. Clemons, *The Marine Corps Way* (New York: McGraw Hill, 2005).

Porter was pleased with the "lessons learned" meeting, prior to the review. In general, the talk with the translation team focused on the work itself, and was based on facts captured in the most recent A3. Several recommendations for further improvement had been proposed.

The actual review meeting was anticlimatic. Nonetheless, it continued to spur more learning for Porter.

During the review meeting he found himself sharing an insight that had only come to him recently. In the beginning, Porter had assumed that gaining traction on the original goals would signal some sort of closure. Instead, he found himself examining the fine details of what was currently working, honing in on why gaps existed between this and a new target state. For the first time, Porter felt that he understood the "continuous" part of continuous improvement. And instead of being discouraged by the unending nature of problems cropping up, he was encouraged by the unending opportunity and challenge.

After the meeting, Porter proposed to create an A3 with a longer-term goal: to build on the improvements to the point where his oversight became unnecessary and coordination handed off to team members. Porter realized that he had created an effective new process, and now his job was to eliminate his job.

Not only would Sanderson continue to rely on Porter, but now that Porter had progressed so well in his own personal learning journey, Sanderson would also monitor how well Porter was mentoring others and creating new problem-solvers. Witnessing others being developed was the most rewarding part of his work.

Plans are things that change.

Hansei—Putting the 'C' in PDCA

"Hansei," which is the Japanese term for self-reflection, refers to the continuous-improvement practice of looking back and thinking about how organizational or performance shortcomings might be improved. Formal hansei or reflection meetings may be held at key milestones, such as the end of a project, to identify problems, develop countermeasures, and communicate the improvements to the rest of the organization so mistakes aren't repeated. Informal hansei can occur daily. Hansei is a critical part of lean operational learning along with kaizen and standardized work.[5]

Developing the capability to practice productive hansei is one of the key traits of lean organizations—and a key to enduring learning. Such core disciplines enable a company to develop what Toyota scholar Takahiro Fujimoto labels an "evolutionary learning capability." Many firms have practices that capture and share knowledge, making them learning organizations, but Fujimoto argues that Toyota's combined practices make it the exemplar of evolutionary learning. Here's how he describes the institutional capacity to gather information, reflect upon it, and grow as a systematic practice:

> *No matter how successful a company has been, it needs to develop an organizational culture of "preparedness." It must convert both the intended and the unintended consequences of its actions, the lucky breaks and the well-laid plans, the temporary successes and the failures, into long-term competitive routines. ... After all, fortune favors the prepared organizational mind.*[6]

Hansei corresponds to the check/study phase of PDCA. One of the most common and useful hansei practices among American organizations is the After Action Review (AAR). Originally developed and used effectively by the U.S. military, AARs are now routinely practiced by businesses as well.

5. *Lean Lexicon, Version 4.0,* edited by Chet Marchwinski, John Shook, and Alexis Schroeder (Cambridge, MA: Lean Enterprise Institute, 2008).
6. Takihiro Fujimoto, *The Evolution of A Manufacturing System at Toyota* (New York: Oxford University Press, 1999).

Porter's Three-Month Review Agenda

Document Translation Three-Month Review

Key Enabling Actions (from Proposal A3)

	Eval	Status
Vendor processes	◎	Three-step process established, working
Central document-flow tracking process	○	Established, working - Some problems getting through
Standard vocabulary database and templates	△	Development delayed - Difficult getting agreement on terms among Acme specialists - Technical difficulties - IT system compatibility issues - Program glitch delayed development Photos and videos widely applied Usage inconsistent - Some Acme departments using consistently, some not - Some translators using consistently, some not

◎ Exceeds expectations ○ Meets expectations △ Requires some kaizen

Goals	Plan	Actual	Analysis
Volume	2,200 pages	2,200 pages	Planned number of documents completed But overtime and rework required Some documents still delivered late
Cost overtime as % of total hrs. worked	0%	10%	10% O/T caused by rework problem
Delivery % of right document at right time	100%	90%	Many documents returned or delayed due to rework
Quality % rework	0%	10%	Some documents returned Many delayed due to back-and-forth Q&A between translator and creator → Mostly for "job description" documents

Reviewer date 9/20/08 Owner DP

	Countermeasure	Who/When
	Ongoing PDCA	Porter Ongoing
	Tweaking, ongoing PDCA	Porter Ongoing
	Investigation, observe, listen Ask why — nemawashi Countermeasures implemented, back on track Continue to check Investigation, Five Whys, training	Porter, each department Rick, Terry Porter, each department Porter, each department, Ana, each vendor

	Countermeasure	Who/When
	Maintain current overall volume level: Ensure delivery of right document at right time ⟶ Review and improve central traffic control function ⟶ Meeting set for next week (detailed project review)	Porter 9/27/08
	Reduce O/T by reducing rework — see "Quality" below	Same as below ↓
	Improve delivery by reducing rework — see "Quality" below	Same as below ↓
	Temporary placement of resident specialist translators at gemba	Porter: Acme approval Frances: Vendor negotiation Ana: Translator coordination

Toward Better Problems, Better People

As the launch of the new plant approached, Porter recognized that much of the progress realized by the process of his last A3 had indeed created new "problems." And that was a good thing. A better set of conditions by no means meant the work was finished: he saw that each "solution" only uncovered new problems.

For example, many of Porter's peers and direct reports were dutifully following the A3 process. Porter had become so enthusiastic about using the A3 as a tool to initiate new action that he had begun to encourage everyone who had a problem or project to think through the item by using this process. He was surprised at how quickly people took to the tool, and even more surprised when a problem developed.

Sanderson had pointed out to Porter that he and others were occasionally focusing on "getting the A3 right" more than thinking about the process. On several occasions he had seen individuals reject perfectly useful A3 reports written by others because they failed to comply precisely with *supposedly* standard templates.

In those instances Porter would gently remind the individual that the point of the A3 was not to produce a pristine document—but to develop an effective countermeasure and to instill a way of thinking. He made this point by asking questions about the details of the project, and he always sought to lead by example. Most of all, he looked for ways to encourage others to take initiative.

As he reflected on how to achieve this goal, he realized that Sanderson had indeed helped him learn to learn. He had learned to take initiative largely because Sanderson rarely—if ever—provided solutions for him. He had discovered much of what he knew through a constant

Wisdom Doesn't Scale Easily

Sanderson was proud of what Porter had accomplished. He was becoming an effective A3 thinker and developing other A3 thinkers. Sanderson had not only come to value his input on projects, but could see that Porter was learning how to mentor others in this challenging and continually evolving way of thinking.

As he conducted his own hansei over what he had learned, Sanderson recognized that his own A3 thinking had progressed and his use of the A3 process was effectively producing reflective problem-solvers. But it was not perfect. And so how, he asked himself, could it be improved?

The company had enjoyed considerable success and growth, which required developing managers and workers who were fluent in A3 management. Yet as he knew from his experience with Porter, this learning process can not simply happen in a mechanical or linear way. Learning was a dynamic, human process that could be supported, nurtured, and even (to an extent) managed—yet could only happen as fast as individuals could learn from experience.

Sanderson had once heard a simple yet somehow unsettling thought from a seasoned veteran of the company, "The Toyota Production System is just a set of countermeasures designed to achieve the 'lean' ideal." He interpreted this as meaning that nothing—not emphasis on the work at hand. He sought to mentor others in the same manner.

Porter was enthused and wanted to instill A3 thinking in every part of the company. Porter, in fact, had a new A3 on his desk. His success on the translation process had all but eliminated the need for his job. As a result, Sanderson had asked Porter to oversee the quality of the first full production run for the expanded plant.

Porter realized that this was an ambitious challenge that would certainly open up many new problems and conflicts. He would be spending all his time at the gemba, engaged in conversations that would reveal facts only after intense observation, discussion, and hands-on engagement. Only now did Porter see this process—which was one enormous problem that housed many smaller problems inside—as an opportunity for growth and learning. With that in mind, he pulled out a blank piece of A3 paper and wrote his initials in the upper right-hand corner.

even the core practices developed to keep the ideal moving forward—could escape the scrutiny of A3 learning.

Every tool and principle was essentially a countermeasure on the journey of constant improvement. He then saw that his role—his responsibility—was to seek improvements to this powerful and effective practice. With that, Sanderson pulled out a blank piece of A3 paper and wrote his initials in the upper right-hand corner.

Key Questions

- Are you making a conscious effort to use the review process as a way of sharing your A3 learning with your team members and with other individuals?
- Have you captured and communicated the key details of what your team has learned?
- Have you considered a wide set of potential scenarios and consequences of the changes—and developed followup activities to address them?
- Is your A3 theme ripe for another full round of PDCA? Should you turn your staff's attention elsewhere?
- Is your team gaining capability of A3 thinking? Are they bringing problems and ideas forward, or waiting for assignments?
- Are issues and problems being revisited repeatedly? This indicates matters are not being dealt with at the root cause.
- Are staff still jumping to solutions?

A3
Improvement

Conclusion—Learning to Learn

Now that you've learned the A3 format and gone through a template, you can forget them. Rather than a rigid template, think of the A3 as a blank sheet of paper or even a blank whiteboard. Think of the blank A3 as the beginning of a conversation or the embarking on a new project, a new journey. The point of the A3 isn't the paper or the format; it's the process in its entirety.

This book has shared the story of an individual whose learning journey may mirror parts of your own. You saw Porter pass through three key stages of awareness that novice A3 authors frequently experience:

1. Porter jumps to a conclusion and—it happens every time—develops strong emotional attachment to it. This is the way he (your staff?) has always gone about trying to solve problems: a great sense of urgency to come up with a quick, creative solution followed by quick emotional/egoistic attachment to that solution as he or she begins to promote it. The conclusion may or may not be "right" in the sense that it "solves" the immediate symptom or even the deeper problem. At this stage the problem owner is driven primarily by the need to provide a solution. The solution is *his* solution, and Porter felt great pressure to prove that his solution was *right*.
2. Then, Porter discovers that he can simply be an investigator and let the needs and facts of the situation speak for themselves. This epiphany is core to the A3 process, but never easy: It took me much experience and longer than I care to recall before I began to truly "get" this approach. Yet developing this detachment frees the problem-solver—Porter in this case—from both the angst of having to prove he is right all the time and the pressure of always having to have an answer. Once grasped, this understanding is liberating.
3. Finally, Porter finds that there is another stage to his learning. While the objective investigator stance is appropriate during the fact-finding phase of his project, he learns that in the final proposal phase he must shed this newly acquired laissez-faire attitude and synthesize what he has learned in order to decide the course of action he thinks is best. He then must champion that course until and unless facts emerge that indicate another course is better. This means the A3 owner must embody these two characteristics sequentially and simultaneously: *objectively, dispassionately, take your own ego out of the equation while also being a champion, an entrepreneurial owner of your proposal.*

This last phase may sound paradoxical; embracing two extremes. And it is. This is another example of where the A3 approach is both a practical tool but also a way of learning. Instead of limiting one's understanding through an "either/or" mental model, A3s require a "both/and" perspective.

I have been learning about the A3 process for 25 years, from the very beginning of my experience in Toyota City. I was mentored, saw others being mentored, mentored others myself. I debated, coached, cursed, and was cursed at. I came to understand others and caused others to understand me. I learned to get things done, to engage the organization, to garner its resources to effectively get things done. "John, you must use the organization. It is there *for* you. Use the organization as if it were a tool to wield, an instrument to play," my boss implored me. I honestly had no idea what he was talking about at first. But he kept coaching, kept imploring, kept mentoring. And, eventually, I began to see.

To me, the A3 came to embody much more than the simple, powerful tool. It embodies the spirit of lively debate, the establishment of mutual understanding and confirmation of agreement that underpinned everything that I saw occurring in the way in which work took place day to day. There was constant dialogue, frequently—especially if it was important—occurring over a piece of A3 paper. But even if there was no actual A3 paper, the same structure and flavor to the dialogue was almost always there. I've tried to capture some of that spirit in this book. It is that spirit of dialogue, not the piece of paper, which is important.

Eventually, I coached others in the A3 process in my role assisting Toyota as it transferrred its production and management systems to North America in the mid-1980s. We initially did not establish the A3 process in Toyota's North American operations; there was enough to occupy us just trying to get operations up and running. Also, we assumed (incorrectly) that there must be something roughly equivalent to the A3 that would be common in American companies. The "one page memo" and the KISS (keep it simple stupid) acronym were well known, and there were plenty of planning processes and training programs generally available. Since an A3 is nothing more than a piece of paper, we didn't—or at least I didn't—think to try to establish it as a formal work process for our new North American affiliates. It was several years later that we realized we were having serious difficulty in getting local managers to understand and follow PDCA as a thinking and operating process. Then, the most natural thing for us to do was to turn to the A3, which Toyota in North America began to institute more formally in the early 1990s.

My first experience in A3 coaching came when I was transferred from Toyota City to Toyota's Tokyo office in 1988. As part of the Toyota Motor Sales organization (Toyota in Japan was divided into a manufacturing company and sales company from 1950 to 1982), the Tokyo office did not have a strong tradition in the rigorous use of the A3 process.

Following the merger of the two companies in 1982, Tokyo managers were expected to submit proposals to the Toyota City headquarters as an A3 report. To my surprise, many of my Toyota Japanese colleagues in Tokyo were terrible at producing A3s, and I found myself in the strange position of coaching my colleagues on what information to include and how to structure their A3s for effectiveness in communicating with headquarters. I was still a relative novice, though, unlike a more senior colleague who also had recently transferred to Tokyo from Toyota City.

This colleague, Mr. Ono, was a true A3 guru. Late almost every evening, after most employees had left for home, a line of mostly younger employees, all working on various company initiatives, would steadily form in front of and around Ono-san's desk. They were lining up to seek advice on their A3s. Ono was a heavy smoker. His evening desk, in the middle of a huge open office, was obscured by a cloud of smoke. Upon finishing with one person, Ono would look up, and motion the next in line to step up and hand over his A3. Ono would take it in hand; look it over quickly; invariably grimace; and, deepening the already deep furrow of his brow, take a long, deep draw on his cigarette and blow it out one corner of his mouth, the smoke now engulfing Ono, desk, and the young A3 author. At this point Ono would offer his first real reaction, which would range from disdainful scoff to derisive guffaw to merciless scorn. He would read the A3 aloud, ignoring the author, just taking in every nuance of what was on the paper, discussing implications, pronouncing simple errors along the way. As he went along and began to understand the business issue in the A3, he would often begin to smile, throwing out observations, asking questions. After about 10 minutes of reading and thinking out loud, he would espouse about 10 minutes worth of comments, by now smiling and having a jovial time, until the end when he would offer a few grave words of advice. Then, next in line. Every night.

Ono wasn't the only one. This type of mentoring was rampant elsewhere in Toyota. It was even built formally into the management development system. Outsiders often assume that Toyota managers are born thinking alike, naturally "on the same page." Nothing could be further from the truth.

When he spoke of "kanban democracy,[1]" Taiichi Ohno was referring to a cultural as well as operational shift that occurs when A3 thinking underlies how people work. Just as kanban cards give *authorization* to either make (production instruction kanban) or move (withdrawal kanban), pull-based authority through the A3 process provides individuals with the authority they need, when they need it. It's as simple as it is powerful.

1. Setsuo Mito, *An Album of a Management Revolution*, (Tokyo: Seiryu Shuppan, 2007).

Indeed, the most important operating function of the proposal A3 is to provide a mechanism for companies to authorize activities, while keeping the initiation of the action in the hands of the person doing the work, the responsible individual. The A3 process is how individuals gain authority and agreement to get the right things done. It forces senior managers to become business owners, and creates the company of experts needed to maintain a gemba-based approach to constant improvement. This is especially important in knowledge-based activities. In factories, responsibility is usually clear, especially for production workers. The challenge is getting people to think. In offices or other forms of knowledge work, where everyone's job is to think, the problem is that responsibility is often muddled.

When you look at how things get authorized in your company, you will find that many specific matters such as line-item spending or policy choices are clearly spelled out. But when it comes to detailing how decisions are made about key operating and even strategic matters, there are probably no clear answers, only a vague notion that everyone is somehow empowered with the requisite authority to accompany their ill-defined responsibility. The result? Responsibility becomes unclear, and the decision-making process breaks down with confusion and frustration vying for dominance. The A3 process provides an elegant and effective means of resolving this issue. Who knows, at any given point in time, what authority is required and what action is necessary? The obvious answer is the person doing the work, the responsible person. The A3 is the instrument enabling the right decision at the right time. *That's why pull-based authority may be the most important JIT element of the entire Toyota system.*

One final word on A3 thinking: The underlying way of thinking reframes all activities as learning activities at every level of the organization, whether it's standardized work and kaizen at the micro/individual level, system kaizen at the managerial level, or major strategic/tactical decisions at the corporate level. All of these processes work in essentially the same way, named and structured differently for different levels of the organization. Problem-solving, continuous improvement, kaizen: Whether inductive or deductive, they are all still based on 1) understanding causality, 2) seeking predictability, and 3) ensuring ongoing, unending learning.

Seeing this underlying way of thinking will help you to avoid getting hung up on the physical format of the A3. The number of A3 types probably roughly equals the number of A3 reports that have been written. There are roughly three (some say four) main "types" of A3 reports for elevating proposals from below, solving problems, and implementing changes, and there are a few templates that have been devised for each of those. But part of the beauty of the process is that it is flexible. The example in this book follows one specific path. Your path will no doubt look different. Examine the examples in the back pocket of this book.

"What about standardization?" you may ask. I think the answer to that question lies in questioning exactly what it is we want to standardize. If we want to standardize specific actions or tasks, then you may wish to provide a standard template and enforce compliance. If, however, you want to induce a rigorous thinking process, a robust problem-solving approach, and encourage and enable individual initiative, then the tool needs to be as flexible and varied as the problems that it is intended to aid in resolving and as diverse as the people who will use it.

Simply, the goal is to embody thorough PDCA rigor in the A3 process, its underlying thinking, and the subsequent actions, and to pursue understanding of causality and attainment of predictability, all while learning every step of the way. Whether contained in an actual A3 report or not, you can begin to think of conversations that contain this thinking as centering around a kind of "virtual A3," where discussants frame their thinking carefully for their listeners, share information to gain mutual understanding with objectivity and respect, and exchange and obtain consensus through vigorous debate as plans are then laid and implementation undertaken. Thorough reflection ensures that the loop is closed, lessons learned, and the process started anew.

Getting Started—It Takes Two to A3

You want to establish the A3 process and A3 thinking in your organization to address problems, propose ideas, and launch projects. How can your organization think and act in accordance with A3 principles? What should you do? Where do you start?

First of all, *start somewhere* and learn from experience. There's no substitute for testing this out with your colleagues, regardless of the setting. And this can only happen by actually creating A3s and working the A3 process. A3 learning takes life only when teams roll up their sleeves, sharpen their pencils, and put this approach to work. When you present your ideas in the form of A3s, expect to be surprised by the reactions and conversations that ensue.

But the A3 process, even initial steps, will require some specific skills for everyone involved; individuals can begin the A3 journey alone by reading this book, studying various problem-analysis tools, or developing a familiarity with many other planning tools. True A3 practice, however, is a team sport.

Once you have dug into the A3 process, be aware that while it's relatively easy for one person to learn how to write an A3, the real challenge of A3 management rests in using one properly. This requires an understanding of the different ways that individuals respond to an A3 at different times. It literally takes "two to A3," interacting in the roles of an author/communicator and a responder/coach, each with a requisite set of skills to be mastered. Individuals within your organization will need to develop the skills of an author/communicator and a responder/coach.

Author/Communicator

The most obvious role to be played in the A3 process is that of the author/communicator. An author is, as we know from reading the journey of Porter, the owner of a problem or challenge. In our story we referred to Porter as the "A3 owner." His first role, though, is to *author* the A3, as opposed to simply *writing* the report. Instead of filling in the blanks in a manner that looks good but doesn't fully satisfy the intent of the format, the author/communicator must develop the knowledge and authority about the problem in order to produce a meaningful proposal.

This requires learning the problem-solving thinking and techniques that are central to the PDCA cycle. In fact, the action and improvement stages of the A3 process rely so fully on this fact-based, problem-solving approach that many managers will ask the author/communicator to produce an interim A3 designed solely to identify root cause—this is what Porter did in Chapter 3. These "interim A3s" or analytic charts help to instill the discipline to avoid jumping to conclusions and solutions (*see Interim A3 Templates pages 124–125*).

Notice that by design interim A3s cut the investigation off after *Analysis*. An author/communicator can then complete his or her recommendation in a full A3, shrinking down the information contained in the interim A3.

The author/communicator also must be able to impart his or her ideas to others. There are two critical aspects of communication. The first is *storytelling*, in which the primary job is to understand the most important theme of the story and to develop the presentation skills of precision and conciseness to communicate it. A storyteller knows how to effectively frame the problem so that it can be better understood in both depth and context by everyone it touches.

The other vital aspect of communication is to be an *advocate*—the person who, after fully investigating the story, takes the discovery to the group in order to implement the best course of action. This is where the skills of nemawashi, negotiation, influence, dialogue, persuasion, and storytelling come into play.

Responder/Coach

Responder/coach is the more difficult of the roles and the source of most failure when using the A3 process. A responder/coach must know *how to read* an A3 effectively, but then move quickly beyond that. The responder/coach, at a given point in time, may be a supervisor, advisor (formal or informal), decision-maker, need-to-know peer, or resource-provider.

Interim A3 Template A—Through *Analysis*

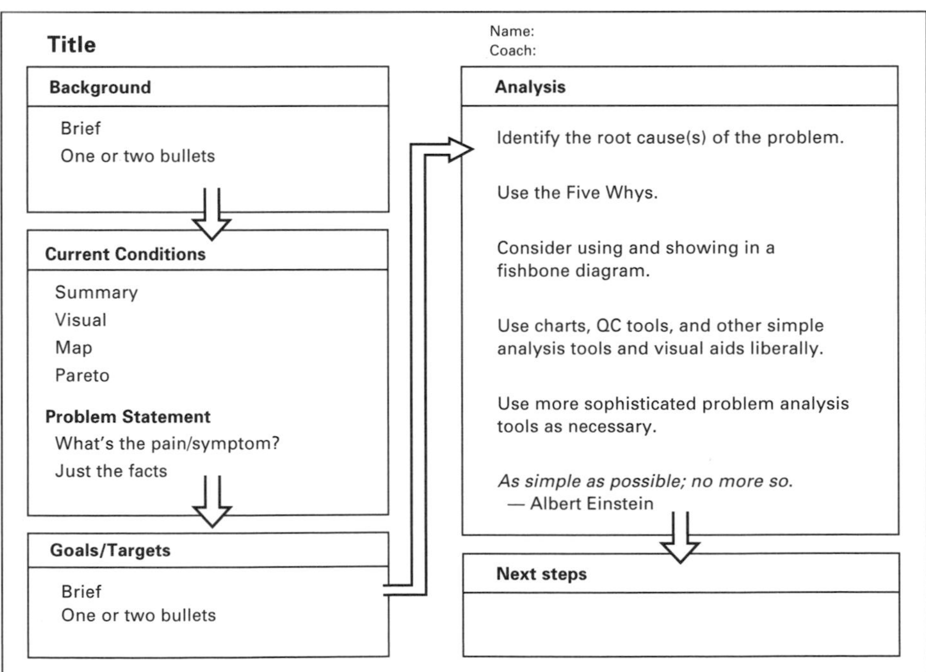

Naturally, the first question that a reader must ask is whether he or she understands what the author is trying to communicate: "Did I understand the story and, most importantly, within that story did I understand the problem?" Having clarity around this business knowledge enables the reader to take on the other portion of their role as coach.

Mentoring and coaching an author on an A3 starts by making sure he or she truly understands his or her own problem. The coach must help the author in seeing that the problem is properly framed, and that the root cause of the problem has been uncovered. The coach must help both the author—and the responder/coach himself—avoid jumping to conclusions. And so no debate about countermeasures should occur until this phase has been worked through completely.

Next, the responder/coach helps an A3 author/communicator by making sure that he or she has developed the best set of countermeasures—and then pushes for a full exploration of the relative merits of each set. Finally, when the author/communicator has earned consensus on the countermeasures, the responder/coach can help him produce a plan of action. Note that in most situations, most of the debate is around "What to do?" followed by frantic focus on "How quickly can we get it done?" If the various participants have followed the A3 sequence of methodical conversation and dialogue, their discussion will have established clear mutual understanding that enables easy and natural agreement on what to do when.

Interim A3 Template B—Through *Countermeasure Selection*

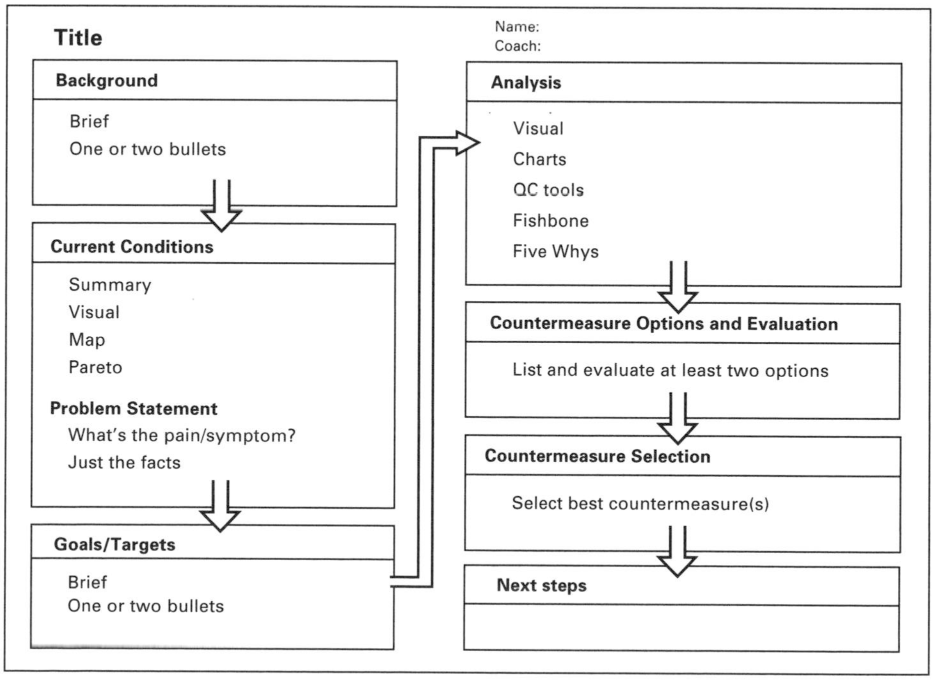

Finally, the responder/coach role entails a deliberate focus on cultivating and sharing lessons learned, as the participants discuss what problems may appear as countermeasures are implemented and how to deal with and learn from them through quick, immediate feedback loops. At this junction, it is critical to foster open communication about the things that might go wrong as well as how to monitor the process. At every stage in the process individuals must remind themselves that teaching others or learning ourselves how to write an A3 is a relatively straightforward matter. Developing the skills to sustain learning is and always will be a constant challenge.

Some Final Dos and Don'ts

Writing an A3 is straightforward, but a few tips can help:

Don't worry about whether to use pen, pencil, or even a computer program: It's amazing how your thinking will become more engaged in the process with the simple thought of putting pencil to paper. Most experienced practitioners prefer to write A3s by hand. However, this is the computer age, and many individuals are more comfortable using computers to create and share A3s over geographic distances.

Don't get hung up on formal elements: The story and format of the A3 should be determined by the specific answers or context of the questions as they relate to the problem or project. Thus, some A3s may have seven boxes, as Porter's does, while others may have four or eight. The author will need to determine the format in each case as he or she works through the process. Some organizations create standard templates and make them available for use on a shared electronic space. This can be a helpful timesaver. The good news is that people will follow this template. The bad news is that people will follow this template. Individuals may become so enamored of "getting the A3 right" that they will shift their focus to producing clean, impressive documents rather than working the problem.

Do get your message across: Effective A3s persuade others by capturing the right story with facts (not abstractions) and communicating the meaning effectively. Make the A3 as easy to read as possible by following a logical flow and allotting space according to importance of items (e.g., more space for analysis or countermeasures that you want to emphasize). Using bullet points rather than sentences and choosing the right visual tools (*see A3 Storytelling Tools on the next page*) can help you effectively condense a lot of information into a small space.

Do get messy: Some of the best A3s are those that have been passed around, marked up, revised, and then passed around, marked up, and messed up again. The more that an A3 prompts healthy debate the more it has done its job. And remember—it doesn't matter if everybody doesn't "speak A3" in order to get started. For everybody to become fluent in this process someone must get started. This may lead to confusion and conflict. If that is the case, you are probably doing something right. The process may be messy, but it works.

Do use the A3 to control meetings: Passing around an A3 and walking through it to guide the discussion is a great way to manage meetings. Instead of allowing conversations to get off track and go down "rat holes," the A3 can assist the meeting owner in keeping things focused.

Do use the A3 to lock down agreements: Capture agreements directly on the A3 in real time as responders say that they are in agreement. Send copies of the agreed-to A3 to all related parties. Bring the agreed-to A3 to subsequent meetings. Of course, individuals can still change their minds, but reference to previously made agreements can make it clear when someone is making an actual change in position.

Do store learnings for later reference and sharing: Computerized databases have their place, but the computer can be a black box, containing so much data that no one knows how to access it in an easily useful way. A3s can serve as practical knowledge-sharing mechanisms since the information—not just data—contained in A3s is contextualized and tells a story.

A3 Storytelling Tools

Section of A3	Storytelling tools	
Background	Graph	Sketch
Current Conditions	Tally sheet Pareto diagram Sketch Current-state map	Histogram Scatter diagram Control chart Graph
Goals/Targets	Chart	Sketch
Analysis	Control chart Relation diagram Tree diagram Sketch Scatter diagram	Cause-and-effect fishbone Histogram Pareto diagram Graph
Proposed Countermeasures	Diagram Sketch Graph	Chart Future-state map Evaluation matrix
Plan	Gantt chart	
Followup	Sketch	Chart

About the Author

John Shook began his observations and analysis of companies, their operations, and organization during his first tour of companies in Japan in 1977. This led to John learning about lean while working for 10 years with Toyota, helping that company transfer its production, engineering, and management systems from Japan to its overseas affiliates and suppliers. This real-world experience in implementing lean principles throughout an organization gives him extraordinary insights into the challenges faced by those who are interested in lean transformation. As co-author of *Learning to See*, John helped introduce value-stream mapping as a tool for lean practitioners; with *Managing to Learn*, he similarly is taking lean practitioners into new territory, that of working with and leading with A3s.

John is an industrial anthropologist who, as CEO of the Lean Enterprise Institute, spends his time researching and developing lean principles and working with companies and individuals to help them understand and implement lean production. He is former director of the University of Michigan, Japan Technology Management Program, and former head of two consulting groups, the Lean Transformations Group, LLC, and the TWI Network, Inc. John is recognized as a true sensei who enthusiastically shares his knowledge and insights within the lean community and with those who have not yet made the lean leap.

Bibliography

Thinking/Problem-Solving

Ackoff, Russell, *The Art of Problem Solving*, New York: Wiley, 1978.

Bateson, Gregory, *Steps to an Ecology of Mind*, Chicago: University of Chicago Press, 2000.

Dewey, John, *How We Think*, Buffalo, NY: Prometheus Books, 1991.

Dorfman, H.A., *The Mental ABC's of Pitching; A Handbook for Performance Enhancement*, Lanham: Diamond Communications, 2000.

Dorner, Dietrich, *The Logic of Failure: Why Things Go Wrong and What We Can Do to Make Them Right*, New York: Metropolitan Books, 1996.

Kranz, Gene, *Failure is Not an Option: Mission Control from Mercury to Apollo 13*, New York: Simon & Schuster, 2000.

Martin, Roger, *The Opposable Mind*, Boston: Harvard Business School Press, 2007.

Petroski, Henry, *To Engineer is Human: The Role of Failure in Successful Design*, New York: St. Martin's Press, 1985.

Petroski, Henry, *Success Through Failure: The Paradox of Design*, Princeton, NJ: Princeton University Press, 2006.

Richards, Chet, *Certain to Win: The Strategy of John Boyd Applied to Business*, Chet Richards, 2004.

Steinberg, Frances, and Whiteside, Richard, *Positive Positioning: How to Get What You Want from Anyone*, Auckland: PHAC Publications, 2006.

Whiteside, Richard G., *The Art of Using and Losing Control: Adjusting the Therapeutic Stance*, Washington, DC: Brunner/Mazel: 1998.

Wiener, Norbert, *The Human Use of Human Beings*, Boston: Houghton Mifflin, 1950.

Organizations

Deming, W. Edwards, *Out of the Crisis*, Cambridge, MA: MIT Center for Advanced Educational Services, 1986.

Drucker, Peter F., *The Effective Executive*, New York: Harper & Row, 1966.

Drucker, Peter F., *Management: Tasks, Responsibilities, Practices*, New York: Harper & Row, 1973.

Drucker, Peter F., *The Practice of Management*, New York: Harper & Row, 1954.

Geus, Arie de, *The Living Company*, Boston, MA: Harvard Business School Press, 1997.

Johnson, H. Thomas, and Broms, Anders, *Profit Beyond Measure: Extraordinary Results through Attention to Work and People*, New York: The Free Press, 2000.

Johnson, H. Thomas, *Lean Dilemma: Choose System Principles or Management Controls —Not Both*, unpublished paper, winner of 2007 Shingo Research Prize Award.

Santamaria, Jason; Martino, Vincent; and Clemons, Erik, *The Marine Corps Way*. New York: McGraw Hill, 2005

Schon, Donald A., *The Reflective Practitioner: How Professionals Think in Action*, New York: Basic Books, 1983.

Senge, Peter, *The Fifth Discipline: The Art and Practice of the Learning Organization*, New York: Doubleday, 1990.

Sloan, Alfred P., Jr., *My Years with General Motors*, New York: Doubleday, 1964.

Weber, Max, *The Theory of Social and Economic Organization*, New York: Oxford University Press, 1947.

Visual Communication

Tufte, Edward R., *The Visual Display of Quantitative Information (Second Edition)*, Cheshire, CT: Graphics Press, 2001.

Tufte, Edward R., *Visual Explanations: Images and Quantities, Evidence and Narrative*, Cheshire, CT: Graphics Press, 1997.

Toyota/Lean Resources

Balle, Michael; Beaufallet, Godefroy; Smalley, Art; and Sobek, Durward, "The Thinking Production System," *Reflections: The SoL Journal on Knowledge, Learning, and Change*, Volume 7, Number 2, 2006.

Fujimoto, Takahiro, *Competing to Be Really, Really Good: The behind-the-scenes drama of capability-building competition in the automobile industry*, Tokyo: International House of Japan, 2007.

Fujimoto, Takahiro, *The Evolution of A Manufacturing System at Toyota*, New York: Oxford University Press, 1999.

Jones, Daniel T., and Womack, James P., *Lean Thinking: Banish Waste and Create Wealth in Your Corporation (Revised Editon)*, New York: Free Press, 2003.

Marchwinski, Chet; Schroeder, Alexis; and Shook, John, eds., *Lean Lexicon (Version 4.0)*, Cambridge, MA: Lean Enterprise Institute, 2008.

Nemoto, Masao, *Total Quality Control for Management—Strategies and Techniques from Toyota and Toyoda Gosei*, Englewood Cliffs, NJ: Prentice Hall, 1987.

Ohno, Taiichi, *Toyota Production System: Beyond Large-Scale Production*, Cambridge, MA: Productivity Press, 1988.

Ohno, Taiichi, *Workplace Management*, Mukilteo, WA: Gemba Press, 2006.

Rother, Mike, and Shook, John, *Learning to See: Value-stream Mapping to Create Value and Eliminate Muda* (version 1.3), Cambridge, MA: Lean Enterprise Institute, 2003.

Spear, Steven, and Bowen, Kent, "Decoding the DNA of the Toyota Production System," *Harvard Business Review*, September-October 1999.

Spear, Steven, "Learning to Lead at Toyota," *Harvard Business Review*, May 2004.

Suzaki, Kiyoshi, *Results from the Heart: How Mini-Company Management Captures Everyone's Talents and Helps Them Find Meaning and Purpose at Work*, New York: Free Press, 2002.

Toyota Motor Corporation Operations Management Consulting Division, *Toyota Production System*, Toyota City, 1992.

Verble, David, unpublished paper.

Ward, Allen C., *Lean Product and Process Development*, Cambridge, MA: Lean Enterprise Institute, 2007.

Ward, Allen; Liker, Jeffrey; Cristiano, John; and Sobek, Durward, "The Second Toyota Paradox: How Delaying Decisions Can Make Better Cars Faster," *Sloan Management Review*, Spring 1995.

Ward, Allen; Liker, Jeffrey; and Sobek, Durward, "Toyota's Principles of Set-Based Concurrent Engineering," *Sloan Management Review*, Winter 1999.

Japan

Abegglen, James C., *The Japanese Factory*, Glencoe, IL: Free Press, 1958.

Abegglen, James C., and Stalk, George Jr., *Kaisha: The Japanese Corporation*, New York: Basic Books, 1985.

Cole, Robert E., *Japanese Blue Collar: the Changing Tradition*, Berkeley, CA: University of California Press, 1971.

Cole, Robert E., *Managing Quality Fads: How American Business Learned to Play the Quality Game*, New York: Oxford University Press, 1999.

Haley, John Owen, *Authority Without Power: Law and the Japanese Paradox*, New York: Oxford University Press, 1991.

Mishima, Yukio, *The Samurai Ethic and Modern Japan: Yukio Mishima on Hagakure*, translated by Kathryn Sparling, Tokyo: Charles E. Tuttle Company, 1978.

Suzuki, Shunryu, *Zen Mind, Beginner's Mind*, Boston: Shambala Publications, 2006.

Whiting, Robert, *You Gotta Have Wa*, New York: Vintage Books, 1990.

Japanese Language Sources

Cho, Fujio, "Toyota Seisan Houshiki—America de no Taiken" ("Toyota Production System—My Experience in America"), a speech delivered to an audience of industrialists in Japan in 1997.

Fujimoto, Takahiro, and Shimokawa, Koichi, eds. *Toyota System no Genten* ("Origins of the Toyota System"), 2001. (Translation forthcoming from Lean Enterprise Institute.)

Kusunoki, Kaneyoshi, *Chosen Hiyaku—Toyota hokubei jigyou tachiage no "Gemba"* ("Challenge: Taking the Leap—On the front lines of establishing Toyota's North American manufacturing presence"), Chubu Keizai Shinbun-sha, 2004.

Mito, Setsuo, *Ohno-san, 21-Seiki mo Toyota seisan housiki ha genki desu yo; 'An Album of an Industrial Revolution'* ("Ohno-san, Your Toyota Production System is doing well in the 21st Century!—An Album of an Industrial Revolution"), Tokyo: Seiryu Shuppan, 2007.

Ohno, Taiichi, *Toyota Seisan Houshiki—Datsu kibo no keiei wo mezashite* ("Toyota Production System—Managing for Leaner Production"), Tokyo: Diamond-sha, 1978. (Available in English translation as "Toyota Production System—Beyond Large-Scale Production" from Productivity Press, 1988.)

Ohno, Taiichi, *Ohno Taiichi no Gemba Keiei* ("Taiichi Ohno's Gemba Management"), Tokyo: Nihon Nouritsu Kyoukai Management Center, 1983/2001. (Available in English translation as "Workplace Management" from Gemba Press, 2006.)

Seiji Yamamoto in Toyota Kuchiguse (Common expressions of Toyota Leaders) by OJT Solutions (Tokyo, Chukei Shuppan, 2006).

Toyoda, Eiji, *Ketsudan—Watashi no Rirekisho* ("Decision—an autobiography"), Tokyo: Nihon Keizai Shinbun-sha, 1985. (Available in English translation as *Toyota: Fifty Years in Motion* from Kodansha International, 1985.)

Feedback

The Lean Enterprise Institute and John Shook have tried make this book easy to understand with a simple storyline and clear examples and A3s. However, we know from years of experience that applying even the simplest concept in a complex organization is difficult. So we need your help. After you have tried working with A3s—as both tools and a management process to build a learning organization—please mail, fax, or email your comments to:

Lean Enterprise Institute
215 First Street, Suite 300
Cambridge, MA 02142 USA

lean.org
Fax: 617-871-2999
Email: info@lean.org

Continue Your Learning

The Lean Enterprise Institute (LEI) has a wide range of learning resources, all with the practical knowledge you need to sustain a lean transformation:

Learning Materials

Our plain-language books, workbooks, leadership guides, and training materials reflect the essence of lean thinking—*doing*. They draw on years of research and real-world experiences from lean transformations in manufacturing and service organizations to provide tools that you can put to work immediately.

Education

Faculty members with extensive implementation experience teach you actual applications with the case studies, work sheets, formulas, and methodologies you need for implementation. Select from courses that address technical topics, culture change, coaching, senior management's roles, and much more.

Events

Every March the Lean Transformation Summit explores the latest lean concepts and case studies, presented by executives and implementers. Other events focus on an issue or industry, such as starting a lean transformation or implementing lean in healthcare. Check *lean.org* for details and to get first notice of these limited-attendance events.

lean.org

A quick and secure sign-up delivers these online learning resources:

- John Shook's thought-leading e-letter delivered monthly to your inbox.
- Use of the Connection Center to network or benchmark with fellow Lean Thinkers.
- Entry to a range of Forums where you can ask questions or help others.
- Access to the Lean Road Map for customizing and tracking a personal learning path.
- Use of the Lean Notebook for saving and sharing important articles.
- First notice about LEI events, webinars, and new learning materials.

About the Lean Enterprise Institute

The Lean Enterprise Institute, Inc. was founded in 1997 by management expert James P. Womack, Ph.D., as a nonprofit research, education, publishing, and conferencing company. As part of its mission to advance lean thinking around the world, LEI supports the Lean Global Network (leanglobal.org), the Lean Education Academic Network (teachinglean.org), and the Healthcare Value Network (healthcarevalueleaders.org).

A3 Examples

Managing to Learn includes a sampling of A3s, which are periodically changed, to illustrate just a few of the formats and themes that may be used.

A3s on lean.org

No one should A3 alone, so please take advantage of the A3 Dojo at **lean.org/mtl** where you can post A3s and receive feedback from an A3 Sensei and other lean community members. You can also see A3s that other people have posted, offer feedback, and ask questions. In addition, all samples A3s ever included in any printing of *Managing to Learn* are available as free downloads on the site.